"Warning that trust in business cannot be restored by regulations alone, Dan Yankelovich proposes an alternative well suited to both realistic executives and concerned citizens."

—David Mathews, Kettering Foundation

"Based on insights gained from decades of in-depth public opinion studies, Yankelovich has marshaled compelling data documenting the decline in public trust in major institutions such as government, business, medicine, and the media. In an effort to reverse this dangerous decline, he focuses on corporations that he believes must take the lead in advocating 'stewardship ethics' as the next phase in the evolution of the corporation for the well-being of both business and society."

—Dorothy Zinberg, Harvard University

"Another brilliant diagnosis and a thoughtful, productive recommendation to deal with a major problem. This creative approach offers real potential for better corporate governance."

—Robert A. Burnett, chairman and CEO (retired),
Meredith Corporation

"As positive and perspicacious as ever, noted public intellectual Daniel Yankelovich urges American corporations to transcend the recent scandals. In crystalline prose, he argues that a higher standard of stewardship ethics will serve the interests not only of big business but also of an increasingly market-driven world."

—Paul W. Drake, University of California, San Diego

"Executives often argue that, in a large corporation, it is impossible to be everywhere. A few bad apples, they suggest, can ruin it for all the good people. Daniel Yankelovich contradicts that false view. Once embraced, stewardship ethics effectively places the CEO and all management everywhere—all the time. The book reviews and reveals the process—and the key."

—Sidney Harman, executive chairman, Harman International,
and author of *Mind Your Own Business*

"*Profit with Honor* is an extraordinary book. Dan Yankelovich not only identifies the reasons why some of America's best-known corporations went wrong, but, more important, provides a road map for all corporations to help society, improve their image, and avoid the sins of the past. Must reading for all CEOs and boards of directors."

—Jack D. Rehm, chairman (retired), Meredith Corporation

Profit with Honor

Profit with Honor

The New Stage of Market Capitalism

DANIEL YANKELOVICH

Yale University Press   New Haven and London

The Future of American Democracy series aims to examine, sustain, and renew the historic vision of American democracy in a series of books by some of America's foremost thinkers. The books in the series present a new, balanced, centrist approach to examining the challenges American democracy has faced in the past and must overcome in the years ahead.

Series editor: Norton Garfinkle.

Set in Minion by Integrated Publishing Solutions, Grand Rapids, Michigan.

Printed in the United States of America by R.R. Donnelley, Harrisonburg, Virginia.

Library of Congress Cataloging-in-Publication Data
Yankelovich, Daniel.
Profit with honor : the new stage of market capitalism / Daniel Yankelovich.
   p.   cm.
Includes bibliographical references and index.
ISBN-13: 978-0-300-10858-3 (cloth : alk. paper)
ISBN-10: 0-300-10858-3 (cloth : alk. paper)
1. Capitalism—Moral and ethical aspects. 2. Business ethics.
3. Social responsibility of business.   I. Title.
HB501.Y364   2006
174'.4—dc22   2005031949

A catalogue record for this book is available from the British Library.

The paper in this book meets the guidelines for permanence and durability of the Committee on Production Guidelines for Book Longevity of the Council on Library Resources.
10   9   8   7   6   5   4   3   2   1

For Barbara, Rachel, Nicole

The behavior of the community is largely dominated by the business mind. A great society is a society in which its men of business think greatly of their functions. Low thoughts mean low behavior, and after a brief orgy of exploitation, low behavior means a descending standard of life.
—Alfred North Whitehead

Contents

Preface: Short Books
and Their Authors

For readers, the great advantage of short books in a harried age is that their time commitment is limited. They can spend their allotment of reading time among a number of books and articles rather than on just a few lengthy treatises.

But short books also have disadvantages. The main one is that their limited length leaves little space for documentation and elaboration. This leaves the reader more dependent on the author's judgment. To some degree, it obliges readers to take the author's assertions on faith. In a longer book, there is greater opportunity to cite sources, to elaborate, to present detailed evidence in support of controversial positions.

Authors of short books are obliged, therefore, to give readers some assurance that their assertions have a solid basis in fact and/or experience. They must present their credentials for inspection. Why should you, as readers, be willing to consider seriously the many claims I make in this book about the current state of business ethics and how they might be upgraded? What assurance can I give you, as readers, that I will serve you as a reasonably reliable guide through the thickets of such an elusive and subtle subject, especially since I am neither a celebrated CEO nor a well-known expert on the subject?

My main qualification as a guide is that I am able to bring the perspective of *privileged witness* to the issue. By "witness" I mean the practical experience of having served on a wide variety of corporate boards of directors and trusteeships—fifteen or so—over a period of thirty years. (For a complete list of these boards and trusteeships, see the Appendix.) These boards frequently encountered the sorts of ethical dilemmas discussed in the chapters that follow. I have been steeped in the practical experience of having struggled with these kinds of ethical issues in a number of different settings, companies, industries and not-for-profit enterprises.

Often, I felt out of place on these boards. Many of my fellow board members were CEOs of other large corporations, bankers, corporate attorneys and accountants. My background and professional qualifications were quite different. I am a social scientist and researcher whose work involves analyzing public opinion and tracking social/cultural trends. In this capacity, I acted as research consultant to many corporations in addition to those on whose boards I served. On these boards I was privileged in the sense of bringing a distinctive and special perspective to bear. The perspectives of business executives and of social scientists like me differ markedly. Not surprisingly, my viewpoint often diverged from that of my fellow directors. To "diverge from" does not necessarily mean "to disagree with." Most of the time, it simply meant that we saw events from different standpoints. Diversity of perspectives is essential in resolving troublesome issues. It prevents groupthink, which I have come to believe is the main enemy of sound judgment on complex issues. To provide such diversity of point of view was one reason I was invited to serve on these boards.

There are many experienced corporate board members qualified to write this sort of book, just as there are many equally qualified social scientists. But there aren't many individuals who straddle both worlds. It is that experience of having straddled both the corporate and the social science worlds for decades that gives me the confidence to plunge into so controversial a subject and to offer what I believe are a number of sound practical recommendations.

A number of people contributed significantly to the style, the substance, and the research underpinnings of this book. First and foremost is my gifted wife, Barbara Lee, whose research skills gave the book a concreteness of examples and a depth of documentation it otherwise would not have had. And I want to acknowledge the invaluable help of my business associate Isabella Furth, who made important contributions to the preparation and drafting of the manuscript.

A number of my friends, all apparently endowed from birth with critical judgment, helped me to maintain a sense of balance and kept me from going overboard on a number of subjects about which I have grown cranky. I want to express my gratitude to Professor Emeritus Robert Weiss, of the Harvard Medical School, and University of California, San Diego, Professors Peter Gourevitch, Michael Schudson, and Sandy Lakoff for reading the full text and giving me the benefit of their understanding of the social/political/historical context in which the changes I recount in the book have taken place. I am also grateful to other friends, associates, and family members—Norton Garfinkle, Laura Nathanson, Nicole Mordecai, Steve Rosell, T. George Harris, Ruth Wooden, Hershel Sarbin, Arthur White, Leon Shapiro, and Dorothy Zinberg—who read the manuscript, gave me the benefit of their critiques, and added deep insights into the unfolding events of the day. It made writing almost pleasurable.

I want to extend special thanks to another group of friends who bring a unique perspective to the manuscript. They are CEOs with whom I have worked over the years on corporate boards and other projects: Pete Peterson (the Blackstone Group), John Pepper (Procter and Gamble), Sandy Grieves (Ecolab), Sidney Harman (Harman International), Jack MacAllister (US West), Thomas "Mack" McLarty (Arkla), and Robert Burnett and Jack Rehm (Meredith Corporation). All have taken the time and trouble to read the manuscript and to bring their personal experiences to bear on its message, underscoring its urgency and practicality.

Richard Atkinson, former Chancellor of the University of California, and Paul Drake, Dean of Social Sciences at UCSD, gave me valued encouragement from the perspective of their academic experiences.

My editor at Yale University Press, Jonathan Brent, contributed many insightful suggestions for improving the text.

Reagan Espino and Dorothy McCarthy both provided unflaggingly cheerful help with preparing the manuscript.

Profit with Honor

Introduction: How to Profit from the Scandals

The purpose of this short book is to suggest that the business community can turn the scandals of recent years to good use, both for business itself and for the larger society. The scandals have shocked the business sector into realizing that something is seriously wrong with its current practice, and that to regain the trust of the American people it must institute far-reaching changes—or else suffer punitive reforms imposed by government. The most badly needed changes are ethical in character, and taken together they represent a new stage in the evolution of market capitalism.

My main argument in the book is that the time has come for market capitalism in the United States to advance to a new stage of enlightened self-interest. American business needs to develop a new ethic—a coherent set of social norms—both to counteract the forces leading to the scandals and to meet the challenges of the global economy that call upon business to take on many new responsibilities. The good news is that some leading corporations are moving in this direction. The bad news is that most are not.

The vast changes taking place in the global economy make it essential that we evolve to a new stage of market capitalism. Coincidentally, to put the scandals behind us we also need a higher standard of ethical norms. The same set of norms, one that I am calling "stewardship ethics," can serve both purposes. Many years ago, the philosopher Alfred North Whitehead observed that "a great society is a society in which its men of business think greatly of their functions." Whitehead believed that business leaders should broaden the orbit of their concerns from those of their individual company or industry to the society at large. I would like to add that a great society is one in which its business, political, and civic leaders (men *and* women) exercise their leadership within a frame of stewardship ethics.

Once Again, a Perfect Storm

The proliferation of recent business scandals has created a wave of public mistrust of corporate America. The mistrust, in turn, has led to onerous new regulations, to the humiliation and imprisonment of once-admired business leaders, and to an automatic presupposition that the business community is guilty of bad faith. Nowadays, few business leaders are given the benefit of the doubt when their companies run into difficulties. The assumption is, "They must have done something wrong."

The scandals cover a wide swath of corporate behavior. They range from gross criminality (Enron, WorldCom, Tyco, Adelphia), to the petty legal mistakes of Martha Stewart, to the steep fines and embarrassing revelations that have ensnared some of the nation's premier companies, such as Fannie Mae, Citigroup, Merck, AIG, Boeing, Shell, JP Morgan/Chase, and Marsh and McLellan.

Why is our culture suddenly confronted with so much corporate wrongdoing? What are the forces giving rise to the scandals?

As time passes and we gain perspective on the first mega-scandal—the 2001 Enron/Arthur Andersen implosion—the causes for the business scandals begin to grow clearer. The scandals are not the result of a national outburst of greed, contempt for the law, the arrogance of power, or a breakdown in corporate governance, though elements of each are present. The main cause is an extraordinary convergence of three trends, the sort of rare phenomenon that generates what people like to call "a perfect storm."

One trend is deregulation. The rage for deregulation that dominated the 1980s and 1990s had many unintended effects. By removing the legal restrictions that prevent blatant conflicts of interest, deregulation tempted some of the gatekeeper guardians of the public interest to sacrifice the principles of their professions for their own economic gain. Deregulation had the perverse consequence of transforming the gatekeepers—the accounting firms, the investment bankers, the business law firms, the regulatory agencies—into enablers. Instead of saying a firm "no" to questionable business initiatives, many of these supposed watchdogs (like the once highly regarded accounting firm, Arthur Andersen) said instead, "Here's how you can do it and get away with it."

Converging with deregulation is the second trend—the practice of linking the richest part of CEO compensation to the vagaries of the stock market. Tying executive incentives to the price of the company's stock has become common practice. The intention is to align the interests of a company's managers more closely with those of its owners—the company's shareholders. This is the most popular way the economic doctrine known as "shareholder value" has been implemented. In practice, however, rewarding executives with stock options potentially worth tens of millions of dollars on top of rich salaries and bonuses has proven to be a debasement of the theory. With such huge sums of money at stake, the company's executives are sorely tempted to take questionable shortcuts, or even to cheat. The pressures on a CEO to put the short-term price of his company's shares ahead of the long-term interests of the company, its employees, and the society as a whole become almost irresistible.

The third and more intangible trend is the steady importation of social norms from the larger culture into corporate life. Ironically, American business, whose deepest tradition is rooted in the ethic of enlightened self-interest, now finds itself caught up in a frenzy of *un*enlightened self-interest. Traditional enlightened self-interest led business executives to search for strategies that benefited others as well as themselves. But the cultural norms of recent years celebrate an ethic of winning for oneself—a zero-sum social Darwinian conception of winning under which if I win, you lose. Fear of the consequences of losing is part of this outlook, as is an offhand attitude toward "gaming the system." Many of today's business executives consider it a challenge—and fun—to find ways to manipulate the system for their own personal benefit.

The convergence of these social norms from the general culture with the business norms of deregulation and the perversion of shareholder value creates conditions for the perfect storm. Combining these forces invents a machine for scandal. Their convergence made the scandals almost inevitable.

What Is the Cure?

It would be a great relief to say that now, in the light of our experience with so many scandals, our business sector is finally taking the right medicine to cure itself. But unfortunately, this is far from the case. The medicine we *are* taking—a heavy dose of legal and regulatory actions—may be necessary, but it is far from sufficient.

Laws and regulations by themselves do not ensure compliance. One of the most prominent features of the scandals is gaming the system—finding clever ways of circumventing the rules and regulations. Accounting and financial management firms seek ways to "smooth" earnings and get around strict accounting standards. Law firms quickly come to understand that legal counsel advising against a questionable course of action wins them scant business or applause. A law practice prospers only when its attorneys are able to advise their clients how they can maneuver their way around the law. Without a normative climate that encourages compliance with laws and regulations, clever people will be tempted to skate on ever-thinner ice—and risk falling through it.

History shows that you cannot fight bad norms solely with laws. The failure of Prohibition in the 1920s—the doomed effort to use the law to prevent people from consuming alcoholic beverages—is only one case in point. The recent scandals present us with a lethal combination of bad norms and bad regulations. The key to successful reform is to combine regulations and norms in such a way that they mutually support each other in encouraging companies (and gatekeepers) to do the right things, not the wrong ones.

Sometimes we do need to resort to legal remedies. Some scandals feature serious violations of the law calling for serious punishment. Few would argue that Bernie Ebbers, the founder of WorldCom, does not deserve his prison term. But most of the scandals—the rip-offs, the conflicts of interest, the "creative accounting"—constitute ethical rather than criminal violations. Our society is already too long on legal approaches to problems and too short on ethical ones. The legal/regulatory side of business, however important, can neither fully account for the scandals nor prevent them in the future. Only a transformation of ethical norms, supported by the right kind of regulation, can do so.

The concept of norms plays a major role in this book. Norms are social values—the unwritten rules that dictate what sorts of behavior are acceptable or unacceptable. Norms refer both to standards for acceptable behavior and to punishments meted out to those who violate the standards. Norms are often specific to particular social roles or subcultures. Every individual is subject to a wide variety of norms that overlap and sometimes conflict. In general, though, norms tend to cohere. A coherent set of norms constitutes an ethic: a generalized way of understanding one's relation to others in a tightly organized polity and society.

My focus on norms is not intended to detract from the importance of the legal/regulatory side of business. But just tightening the law, throwing some high level executives in jail, and changing the governance rules of boards of directors, however desirable or necessary, will not be sufficient to raise the level of corporate ethics. To counteract the scandals, the normative side of business must receive priority at the same time that the legal side is being strengthened.

My emphasis on norms differentiates this book from most recent writing on the corporation. Over the past forty years much scholarly work on the corporate sector has focused on corporate governance—the legal and regulatory mechanisms for managing the problems that arise from the conflicting interests of various stakeholders, especially the separation of corporate ownership and control. Business corporations have always stirred up conflict and legal dispute because the stakes are so high. The stakes concern money and power and influence and issues of control—things people fight about. In democracies, the law often settles the fights. Scholars therefore write about contracts and regulations and legal disputes. Recently, some noted scholars have added politics to the mix, because decisions about what gets regulated and enforced are often the product of political struggle. As the political scientist Peter Gourevitch observes: "It is no wonder . . . that corporate governance provokes conflict. . . . Anything that shapes wealth, opportunities, stability, and corruption is sure to attract the concerns of the powerful and provoke the anxiety of the weak. Everyone has a stake in the corporate governance system, and everyone has an interest in how it is structured. . . . We believe that corporate governance structures are fundamentally the result of political decisions."[1]

But the law is a blunt instrument, especially when it is the product of political negotiation, and there is only so much that government can do to influence corporate behavior. Efforts to combat ethical shortcomings with legal restrictions emphasize blame, constraints, fines, jail sentences, and other negativities. If you want positive results, you need to give people a positive basis for trust and respect and an ethical vision to live by, not merely severe punishments for misdeeds. The law can't inspire the far-sighted corporate leadership that is so badly needed. It can't enhance the contribution that the business sector can and should make to the larger society. To achieve these broader goals, we need to look to the cultural and human side of corporate life—to the values and motivations and belief systems of people.

There is nothing novel about this emphasis. Way back in 1932, in their classic work on the corporation, Adolf Berle and Gardiner Means spoke of their fear that "power, prestige or the gratification of professional zeal" might distract managers from their main task of making money for the company's shareholders.[2] Add to these such newer temptations as the sheer magnitude of the rewards for cheating (tens of millions of dollars) and the powerful rationalization that as long as you aren't breaking the law, you aren't doing anything wrong. These are not legal matters; they are matters of values and ethical norms.

Business scandals constitute just one symptom of normative confusion in the nation. There are countless others—the troubles of the Catholic Church, the blind spots of the Congress in budget making, the corruptions of state and city government, the muddled priorities of the American Red Cross, even baseball's steroid scandals.

I have chosen to focus on ethical confusion in the business sector for one reason above all others: I believe that the chances for success are better here than in other spheres of American life, and that a high standard of ethical clarity in the business sector will help to dispel moral confusion in the culture at large. In our country, the business sector occupies a role of centrality and prestige. As the source of our economic well-being, its health and vitality are immensely important to Americans. Just yesterday, CEOs like G.E.'s former chairman, Jack Welch, Chrysler's Lee Iacocca, and Intel's Robert Noyce were culture heroes, models to emulate. If business gets its ethical act together, it may well serve as a model and inspiration for others to do the same.

The four-hundred-year history of the limited liability corporation is replete with scandals, reforms, abuses, midcourse corrections, and redirected energies. The present moment gives the business sector a splendid opportunity to transform scandal, embarrassment, and mounting public mistrust into revitalized ethical standards that will be good for business, good for the nation, and good for the world.

Capitalism has always been a work in progress, never a finished product. Marxists have always underestimated the flexibility of capitalism and its ability to adapt to changing circumstances. The father of modern capitalism in the eighteenth century, Adam Smith, was a moral philosopher, attributing to human nature an inborn empathy for others. It was this presupposition that gave credibility to his master concept of "the invisible hand," which made the economic pursuit of self-interest compatible with the interests of the larger society in what Smith called a "society of perfect liberty."[3] Capitalism has always aligned itself with this concept of enlightened self-interest. The key question—the one that dominates this book—is how best to apply it to our own historical era.

Potentially, our nation's prospects for upgrading corporate ethical standards are quite good, for two reasons. One is rising expectations from outside the business sector; the other is a growing urge for reform within the business sector itself.

Business leaders are growing more aware that new expectations are in the air. In the words of Samuel Palmisano, CEO of IBM: "All businesses today face a new reality. . . . Businesses now operate in an environment in which long-term societal concerns—in areas from diversity to equal opportunity, the environment and workforce policies—have been raised to the same level of public expectation as accounting practices and financial performances."[4]

In a statement published in the April 7, 2005, *New York Review of Books,* Lee Scott, the CEO of Wal-Mart Stores, defended the giant retailer against its critics. Wal-Mart is a gigantic enterprise: it employs a million people; in 2004 its sales exceeded $260 billion. The final paragraph of Scott's two-page ad illustrates a business awakening that is still at a very early stage. Scott writes: "To be honest, most of us at Wal-Mart have been so busy minding the store that the way our critics have tried to turn us into a political symbol has taken us by surprise. But one thing we've learned from our critics . . . is that Wal-Mart's size and industry leadership mean that *people expect more from us. They're right to, and when it comes to playing our part . . . we intend to deliver*" (emphasis added).

Cynics may sneer at Wal-Mart's newfound religion and dismiss it as mere public relations—empty rhetoric covering hard-core hypocrisy. And so, indeed, it may turn out to be. But it may also turn out to be a far more benign phenomenon, a sign of responsiveness to changing expectations. Typically, responsiveness starts with a change in corporate attitudes at the leadership level, followed eventually by a significant change in corporate behavior.

We *do* expect more from the giant multinational corporations of our era. Under the right conditions they *can* deliver. We look to Toyota and other car manufacturers to lessen our energy dependence; BP, Shell, and other oil companies to search for alternative fuels and practical remedies to the threat of climate change; G.E., Procter and Gamble, and other giant international companies to open new markets in developing nations; General Motors and other large employers to help resolve the health care crisis; Citigroup and other financial institutions to address the capital needs of poor people in developing nations; Microsoft and other technology companies to digitize the world; the corporate sector in general to assist poor nations in securing the training, education, and resource management they need to enter the global economy.

The challenge to business is, in part, a matter of responding to these heightened expectations. Only a small number of businesses are currently responding well to the challenge. Many more are capable of responding skillfully and effectively.

Ethical Stirrings within Business

My decades of research on American attitudes and values have led me to the conclusion that existing standards of business ethics are too weak to stop the scandals and restore trust. Our corporations need to adopt a higher standard of ethics.

The corporations I have worked with personally (either as a board director or consultant) operate at several levels of ethical standards. The lowest level is one in which the legal department is consulted to make sure that the company is not breaking any laws, or at least none whose violations might get them caught. The next level up is the ability of company policies and actions "to pass the smell test"—a term of art in business circles to refer to proposals that meet minimum legal requirements but fail to adhere to the society's conventional ethical standards. In many companies, there is at least one board director who can be counted on to say in response to a fishy-sounding proposal, "Well, maybe it's legal, but it doesn't pass the smell test." More than half of the companies I have worked with use the smell test as their everyday ethical working guide to action.

Figure 1 illustrates the hierarchy of current ethical standards in the business sector. The lower two-thirds of the pyramid reflects the dominant mores—staying within the law and passing the smell test. The top one-third symbolizes a higher standard of ethical norms.

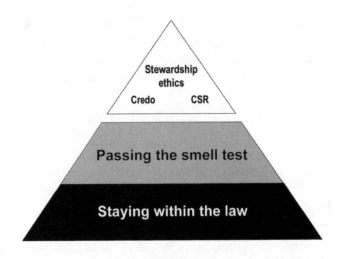

Figure 1. The hierarchy of ethical standards

In the wake of the business scandals, increasing numbers of companies are seeking to achieve the higher standard represented by the top third of the pyramid. The most traditional way of pursuing that goal is by way of a company credo—often articulated by the company's founder and maintained by his successors. Some companies faithfully live by such credos and internalize them within and throughout the company. Enron, which famously touted its high-minded credo, has cast a shadow over the practice of publicizing company credos. But companies like Johnson and Johnson with long-established credos see Enron as a symptom of flagrant hypocrisy and stick by their own tradition.

The Corporate Social Responsibility movement (CSR) represents a more recent form of striving toward higher ethical standards. For a variety of reasons spelled out in subsequent chapters, CSR has not caught on in corporate circles as well as its advocates hoped it would. The early advocates of CSR in the 1960s, 1970s, and 1980s came mostly from the non-business segments of society. They spoke in the off-putting accent of moral superiority, and they betrayed ignorance of business realities, making demands that threatened to weaken the competitive positions of companies. Moreover, their tactics were often self-defeating: they would target the most responsive companies, returning with new demands to the same company again and again, causing these companies to feel like fools for responding so readily.

CSR's biggest liability was that its early proponents had a deeply ambivalent attitude toward corporate profits. Many of them wanted to see companies that followed CSR principles make a profit, but profit making was a secondary consideration, and for some barely an afterthought. To put it mildly, this tendency limited CSR's appeal to the corporate sector.

In this earlier period of CSR's existence, the philanthropic activities of most companies consisted of writing a check (sometimes quite a fat one, as in Mobil's sponsorship of *Masterpiece Theatre*). The marketing guru Philip Kotler points out that CSR evolved into a more businesslike enterprise in the 1990s.[5] Many companies that had avoided causes related to their businesses, to avoid appearing to be self-serving, did a 180-degree turn. They focused their involvement on activities of concern to their employees and customers and related to their core businesses—for example, Shell started to cooperate with environmental groups, and Dell began a program of recycling of computers at no cost to purchasers.

The concept of stewardship ethics that I develop in this book puts more emphasis on profit than do most CSR initiatives. My conception of stewardship ethics retains profit making as a top corporate priority. But it takes the further position that, with sufficient effort and the right sort of strategic analysis, the business sector can do a far better job than it has in reconciling profit making with taking better care of its employees, its customers, its community, and the larger society. As CSR evolves, it is likely to overlap with stewardship ethics more than it has in the past. But the emphases of the two codes of ethics are different. With its roots outside the business sector, the interests of CSR will naturally focus on the social good that corporations can do, irrespective of their profitability; stewardship ethics will focus on decisions that advance the good of the company. When General Motors had a choice years ago to invest its capital either in acquiring Hummer or in making more fuel-efficient vehicles, it chose Hummer. In retrospect, it would have been far better off today if it had made the business (and existential) choice that devotion to stewardship ethics would have dictated.

There is nothing novel about the concept of stewardship. The word is familiar to almost everyone, though it has a variety of meanings. Many businesses trot it out around Christmastime, as if it were too special to pursue every day. Churchgoers sometimes wince at the mention of stewardship because it usually means "give money now." Stewardship is also used frequently in discussions of the environment, where it has the literal and religious connotation of caring for, restoring, and improving the water, air, forests, oceans, land, animal habitats, and other parts of the physical environment so essential to nature's well-being.

In this book, I use the term *stewardship ethics* to convey the commitment to care for one's institution and those it serves in a manner that responds to a higher level of expectations. In the chapters that follow, I elaborate how the ethical commitments of corporate cultures are directly related to the social, political, and economic structures of the larger society. If our corporations can upgrade their ethical norms to the level of stewardship ethics, this achievement will also strengthen the ethical values of our society.

It is prudent to avoid ranking company credos, CSR, and stewardship ethics in hierarchical order of ethical standards. Each has its own strengths and limitations. But whether through taking company credos more seriously, or through accepting CSR principles, or through adopting stewardship ethics (as I propose in this book), it is the space in the pyramid above the smell test that is attracting the attention of more and more corporations.

The Wider Context

If our society expects business to be more engaged in the larger problems and concerns of our times, we need to understand what those concerns are, especially ones that are unfamiliar and even startling. Though we are in only its first decade, the twenty-first century is already shaping up as strikingly different from the previous one. In the twentieth century, nation-states with highly organized military forces fought with one another over issues of balance of power, colonialism, and territory. The major ideological struggle was Marxism versus capitalism.[6]

The tensions and struggles of the current century have a far different character. Colonialism is mostly past. Balance of power and territory have grown less important, ideology more important. But unlike in the past, ideology is not mainly about capitalism and economics. Instead, it is about religion, culture, and social morality. The West is engaged in a bitter ideological struggle with Islamic fundamentalism that focuses on essential values and cuts across national boundaries.

Western leaders have made a conscious effort to avoid framing the struggle as a religious war or a clash of civilizations. But its religious fervor and intensity are hard to avoid. This ideological/religious struggle is in turn taking place in a global economy that creates ever-larger gaps between have and have-not nations—at the same time that it opens up new opportunities for the have-nots to join the haves. The several billion people in the world who live on less than two dollars a day want to join the club of prosperous market economies. Thanks to technology and advances in market capitalism, the means actually exist for them to do so—a shift that will give a giant boost to world economic growth. Technology is helping people to live longer. It is making communication easier. And it shows promise of developing technological fixes for some of the globe's most bewildering problems, such as adapting to climate change, finding substitutes for fossil fuels as sources of energy, and creating abundant supplies of fresh water and food.

In the midst of these varied global changes, the American public has become absorbed in, and distracted by, a struggle to rediscover its own ethical bearings. A muddy ethical confusion pervades the culture, and Americans increasingly turn to religion for guidance. Opinion polls show that Americans are turning to religion in their quest to find firmer ethical ground on which to stand.[7] The United States' cultural revolution, initiated in the 1960s and 1970s, made our society more tolerant, more pluralistic, and freer. But these positive developments have had unintended consequences. They have led to a disorienting moral relativism and difficulty in distinguishing between right and wrong.

On the political front, conservatives, liberals, and moderates all worry about the loss of moral rectitude in our society. Conservatives focus on family-linked issues like abortion, gay marriage, and a morally toxic environment in which to bring up children. The more liberal-minded have a different set of outrages: the ever-expanding gap between rich and poor, threats to the environment, corporate executives enriching themselves by ripping off others, and the ethics of a might-makes-right foreign policy that alienates traditional allies and engenders fear and hatred of the United States in other parts of the world.

Perhaps the clearest sign of ethical confusion in the nation is the proliferation of so-called unsustainable trends—the increasing din about the lack of "sustainability" of our present policies. Within the space of a week or so I have heard or read that . . .

- Our Social Security system is unsustainable
- The rising tide of health care costs is unsustainable
- Our swelling trade deficit with other nations is unsustainable
- The trend toward a weaker dollar is unsustainable
- Our energy policies and dependence on Middle East oil are unsustainable
- The widening gap in our society between rich and poor is unsustainable
- Our frayed relations with our traditional allies are unsustainable
- Our policy of stonewalling the efforts of other nations to do something about climate change, with its threat of global warming, is unsustainable
- The growing political polarization between the "red states" and the "blue states" is unsustainable
- Our policies toward the Muslim world, with their implicit threat of igniting a religious war, are unsustainable

• The poor performance of our students on math tests in relation to students from other nations is unsustainable

Our nation rose to greatness because we are a resourceful people blessed with a practical-minded, pragmatic, nonideological political culture—and a gift for problem solving rather than theorizing. There is nothing inherently overwhelming about these so-called unsustainable trends if we confront them with our customary pragmatism, practicality, and core American values.

What is most depressing about the current political scene is that we seem to have abandoned our habit of facing issues head-on. We are flooded with problems to which we are unresponsive. In place of wise and responsible leadership, we get denial and avoidance, pandering to wishful thinking, ideological conviction posing as thought, short term-itis, polarized politics, a loss of moral compass, infatuation with technical fixes for nontechnical problems, mythical silver bullets, simple-minded sound bites. What a strange turn of destiny it is that when we most need our traditional practicality, we decide instead to overdose on superficiality, ideological willfulness, and inadequate solutions. Situations don't start out unsustainable; they become so when they fester for too long. The more we neglect them, the worse—and less sustainable—they become. Until and unless we regain our sense of ethical direction, our moral compass, we will not be able to cope with all the forms of unsustainability that confront us.

Throughout the nation, these varied concerns hover in the back of most people's minds as a vague and anxious-making suspicion that something has gone wrong in America, without a clear and cogent diagnosis of what it is.[8]

At first glance, these broader concerns may seem unrelated to the subject of this book—the quest for a new ethic for business. But a deeper look shows that they are directly relevant. The key question for the United States is what institutions are best equipped to address the key issues confronting the present century—the cultural/ideological war with Islamic fundamentalism, the need for sustainable development, climate change, the expansion of market economies to the developing world, the harnessing of technology to achieve energy independence, and so on. The assumption that our government and our educational and religious institutions can and will address these issues is unrealistic if we assume that government can do what needs to be done without heavy reliance on the resources of the business sector.

To open the developing world to market economies we need the direct engagement of corporate America. To create customers for our products, we need to support large-scale efforts to raise education levels throughout the globe. To grope our way toward energy independence, to deal with climate change, to raise the level of global health and combat infectious diseases, to create new opportunities for women—for these and other vital tasks we need the participation and support of our powerful multinational corporations. Corporate America may also prove essential to prevailing in our struggle with Islamic fundamentalism. To win the support of Muslim moderates and isolate the extremists, we may need farsighted economic programs, not primary reliance on military force.

The late Roberto Goizueta, former CEO of the Coca-Cola Company, put the point pithily: "While we were once perceived as simply providing services, selling products and employing people, business now shares in much of the responsibility for our global quality of life."[9] This is the heart and soul of the next stage of market capitalism. The right kind of enlightened self-interest for the new century is the one that companies like Coca-Cola, Procter and Gamble, G.E., Starbucks, Shell, and others are moving toward: a broader engagement in solving our most obdurate global challenges.

Part I
Framing the Problem

I

The Wrong Way
to Stop the Scandals

The new century started with some heavyweight business scandals. Enron and its CEO, Kenneth Lay, Tyco and its CEO, Dennis Kozlowski, WorldCom and its CEO, Bernie Ebbers—in each case, colorful men, gifted with more than a touch of good old American con artistry, had apparently enlisted the aid of younger men with specialized accounting skills to cook the books. It took years of trials and mistrials and bald-faced denials and evasive legal maneuvering for their cases to move to the courts. Only the decades of sexual abuses in the Catholic Church—and the hefty fines the church paid to get out from under the resultant scandals—proved a greater shock to the public.

Among the business scandals, Enron topped all others. The Enron story unfolded in slow motion, a miasma of complex financial detail obscuring its full scope. It took a long time for the extent of Enron's apparent fraud (abetted by its accounting firm, Arthur Andersen) to reach full public consciousness. But when it did, the one fact that stood out most vividly in the

minds of observers throughout the nation was that the big
boys had enriched themselves while the savings of loyal employees and small stockholders were wiped out.

In the months following the outing of these and other al-
leged accounting scandals, most business executives continued
to plead the "few bad apples" defense. They acknowledged
(how could they not?) that the gaming tactics of Enron and its
accountants were out of control. But they put the blame on a
handful of rogue companies and personalities, vehemently
denying that the abuses were systemic.

The public, on the other hand, never bought into the
"few bad apples" story. By wide margins, average citizens saw
the abuses as more general. In July 2002 a *Wall Street Journal*
poll found that fewer than one in five Americans thought the
scandals were confined to a "few bad apples." The same month
a *CBS News* survey reported that two-thirds of the public believed that most corporate executives were dishonest, *Newsweek* found that almost seven out of ten put the blame for the
scandals squarely on the shoulders of corporate executives,
and a *Business Week*/Harris survey discovered that 79 percent
believed that "most corporate executives put their own personal interests ahead of employees and shareholders."

But even the skeptical public was unprepared for the
flood of scandals that followed in the next few years. Enron,
WorldCom, and Tyco had involved out-and-out chicanery.
The scandals that followed described a different kind of corporate malfeasance, involving less blatant violation of the law.
Instead, we saw instance after instance of conflicts of interest
that may have stayed within the letter of the law but certainly
flunked the smell test. Hardly a day has passed without news
stories of ethically challenged corporate behavior, especially
on Wall Street. Some of the nation's—and the world's—largest,

most successful, most highly respected corporations found themselves squirming in the media spotlight as they attempted to defend highly questionable actions.

A Day's Worth of News Coverage

In later chapters, we will look more closely at some of these companies. For present purposes, let us take a quick snapshot of an average day's news as reported in the *Wall Street Journal* and the *New York Times*. We might have picked any day at random. For this exercise, I picked December 16, 2004. The date has no special significance.

Here is what these two national newspapers reported on that day in the field of finance:

- The head of the Securities and Exchange Commission ruled that the giant mortgage finance company Fannie Mae had violated accounting rules and must restate its earnings.
- Time Warner settled two separate complaints against its AOL division. In one, the Justice Department agreed to defer prosecution on securities fraud charges provided that AOL operates under strict oversight. The *Times* reported that the three executives named in this complaint "have agreed to cease violating securities laws but can remain in their current posts and will pay no penalties."
- The insurance broker Marsh and McLellan closed a $3 billion credit agreement with a variety of banks that had withdrawn their financing in the wake of charges of bid rigging and kickbacks.

- In the WorldCom class action suit, a judge rejected investment banks' efforts to have the case thrown out. The banks had claimed that they did not need to notify investors of their own reservations about WorldCom securities because they had an auditor's report indicating that the company's financial statements were accurate. The judge rejected this argument and the case went to a jury.
- The federal Pension Benefit Guaranty Corporation, which insures companies' pension plans, discovered that it faced a huge shortfall. The problem arose because the system encourages companies to make risky investment decisions and pass losses on to the pension guaranty agency.
- Morningstar, a research firm that rates mutual funds, was under investigation by the SEC and the New York attorney general on allegations that its advice to investors was compromised by payments from investment companies.
- First Command Financial Services agreed to pay $12 million to settle accusations that it used misleading information to sell mutual funds to military officers.
- Tyson and its ex-CEO offered to pay $1.7 million to settle an SEC investigation into improper company perks.
- A former sales director of a biotech company was indicted for offering doctors kickbacks in exchange for writing prescriptions for the company's AIDS drug.
- The doughnut company Krispy Kreme announced that it might need to restate its financial results

for 2003. This was the latest in a string of questions about its accounting practices, which were under investigation by the SEC.

• The New York Stock Exchange banned a floor clerk from the exchange for "front-running" customer orders (leaking word of pending orders to a client). The NYSE head of market surveillance said, "We want to make it crystal clear that at the exchange, the customer comes first."

• Regulators examined whether insiders at Wall Street firms were tipping off favored investors about deals that might cause stock prices to fall.

Nor are ethical lapses confined to business and finance. Here is what was covered in the *New York Times* and *Wall Street Journal* on that same day in some other domains:

POLITICS

• It was announced that one of the principal authors of the new Medicare drug law would become president of the chief lobbying organization for drug companies. Critics decried this as another example of the revolving door between government and industry.

• Revelations continued in Bernard Kerik's aborted nomination to head the Department of Homeland Security. Incredibly, Kerik's problems—which ran the gamut from debt to multiple extramarital relationships to possible mob connections—had not been spotted by White House or New York City investigators. A commentary piece concluded that political favoritism had blinded the watchdogs from doing their job. Another article examined the possibility that the undocumented nanny who provided the pretext for Kerik's withdrawal from consideration might not actually exist.

- A high-level weapons buyer in the U.S. Air Force admitted to awarding billions of dollars in contracts to Boeing at the same time that she was secretly negotiating with the company for jobs for herself and members of her family.

- Several former military lawyers decried attorney general nominee Alberto Gonzales's memos supporting the use of torture in interrogating terrorism suspects. They maintain that these memos, and Gonzales's claim that the president is not bound by international or federal laws banning torture, opened the door to widespread abuse of prisoners in Afghanistan, Iraq, and Guantánamo Bay.

SPORTS

- The New York State Police raided several racetracks and seized documents as part of an investigation into weight rigging and jockey misconduct.

- A University of Tennessee football player was dismissed from the team for cheating on a drug test, which he failed. "I just never thought I would get kicked off the team," the player said. "I always thought it would work out."

- An outfielder for the Los Angeles Dodgers began serving a jail sentence for driving away while a police officer was writing him a speeding ticket.
- The founder of the Bay Area Laboratory Co-operative (BALCO) was under investigation by the International Olympic Committee for providing steroids and other performance-enhancing drugs to elite athletes.
- In an op-ed piece, a journalist reported that the scandal, corruption and win-at-all-costs ethos that plagues professional and college sports is now trickling down to the high school level.

ENTERTAINMENT

- A British production company filed suit against the Fox television network, claiming that the Fox reality series *Trading Spouses* was in fact a blatant copycat of the British company's hit series *Wife Swap*.

This cross-section of a single day's news coverage depicts the sorry state of the nation's ethical norms as seen through the lens of journalism. When we turn to the nation's response, we see lots of action.

Reliance on Legalism

The main effort to stop the ethical deterioration is taking place in the legal/regulatory domain. Legal authorities have levied huge fines. Well-heeled corporate executives have been forced to resign or to pay some of the fines out of their own pockets.

Some have ended up taking the "perp walk." To produce better financial reporting, Congress has passed stringent new regulations (like the Sarbanes-Oxley Act) that impose a huge accounting burden on business. State prosecutors like New York's Eliot Spitzer have relentlessly tracked down conflicts of interest in the mutual fund and insurance industries. In the overheated drive to make an example of someone, Martha Stewart got tossed into jail for five months—mainly for being a celebrity who happened to trade some shares on inside knowledge and then lied about it. Her transaction involved a few thousand dollars—a piddling sum compared to the many billions of dollars that the real pros bilked from small investors and employees.

These well-publicized legal and regulatory actions momentarily appeased the public. But experts close to the scene do not believe they have done much to remedy the problem. On the PBS program *Wall Street Week with Fortune,* the financial journalist Maggie Maher stated that conflicts of interest on Wall Street routinely persist after all the fines, regulations, and firings. She said flatly, "Mutual funds continue to pay brokers to recommend specific funds." On the same program Edward Siedle, a former SEC enforcement attorney, pointed out that the mutual fund industry is "still allowed to self-regulate, self-adjudicate, self-insure, and even control public access to the criminal and disciplinary action of its membership," with the result that the public thinks that doing business with brokers is much safer than it really is. Siedle observed that "the biggest lesson to be learned in the past few years is that anybody who purports to offer objective advice probably isn't. Most providers of advice have been corrupted, because there is far more money to be made offering tainted advice."

Under a practice euphemistically called "revenue sharing," mutual funds make secret payments to brokers to push their funds. Edward Jones, which operates the nation's largest network of retail brokerage offices (ten thousand sales offices) was fined $75 million and its top executive was forced to resign when it was revealed that its brokers earned posh vacations and cash if they pushed the mutual funds of firms making secret payments to the company. Regulators found that more than 95 percent of Jones's mutual fund sales were of this sort. Maggie Maher asked rhetorically, "Do you really want your brokers to recommend funds because they've been essentially bribed to do so?" And Siedle concluded, "Nothing [on Wall Street] has changed."[1]

In Search of Better Norms

Traditionally, the law marks the border between criminal and noncriminal behavior. Ethical norms, on the other hand, mark the border between right and wrong, without reference to the law. The law is a floor—a foundation on which the norms of the society rest. It is not, and cannot be, a substitute for the ethical norms that sit atop it.

Every viable society depends on ethical norms to guide and restrain conduct. For most forms of conduct, norms are far more important than legal constraints. The law prescribes minimalist standards of conduct—one can act legally and still not act ethically. Ethical norms fill in the blanks necessarily left by the law, which cannot provide a complete blueprint for how individuals or institutions should behave.

In most societies, the legal foundation is relatively thin, while the layer of social ethics that sets the standards for how people and institutions should act is heavier and thicker. Society's legal underpinnings are formal and codified. Its ethical norms are informal and left mostly *un*codified. Even though they may not be written down, however, ethical norms play an indispensable role in the healthy functioning of society.

One consequence of America's cultural revolution in the 1960s and 1970s was a weakening, a thinning out, of its ethical norms. The result is that the ethical standards of today are often put to the minimalist test of whether an action is legal or illegal. Today it is not uncommon to hear the claim: "I didn't break the law, so I didn't do anything wrong." Such a rationale for unethical behavior would have been unthinkable in the 1950s or earlier periods of American life, when society assumed that people's responsibilities encompassed far more than merely satisfying the minimal standard of legality.

The decline in ethical norms is not confined to America's corporate sector. It is also on display in incivility in public places—road rage, obscenity, violent public confrontations—and has led to the proliferation of crudeness, violence, and cheapened sex in popular culture and entertainment.

Most Americans are unhappy about the deterioration of our ethical norms. Opinion polls consistently register the public's desire for a higher level of ethical standards. But we don't seem to know how to go about the task of repairing them.

Our first impulse is to regulate or deregulate or both. Part of the fix we are in can be blamed on relying so heavily on the blunt instrument of the law to fix our ethical problems. There is an important lesson to be learned from the perfect storm. Deregulation combined with looser ethical norms created a storm of bad corporate behavior. Not only did it tempt corporate executives to cheat, it tempted the watchdogs and guardians of the public trust to cheat as well. The results were devastating.

I believe that if we rely primarily on regulatory and legal mechanisms to repair the damage, we will not get very far. We will force the gamesters of the system—clever lawyers and accountants and financial executives—to be more ingenious and more careful. But we will not transform the ethical climate. As a society, we need to develop a better understanding of how to use the law to support higher ethical standards, not as a substitute for them.

II
Screwed Again

Research into the causes of mistrust reveals a sure-fire formula for guaranteeing that you will never be trusted again. Here is what you must do.

- First, you work hard to win the trust of others.
- Then, when you have it, you go back on your word. You lie, you deceive, you play the others for fools.
- Then you seek their forgiveness. You admit you were wrong. You say you have learned your lesson. Slowly, gradually, painfully, you rebuild the bond of trust.
- Then, once you are sure you have regained their trust, you screw them again.

That should do the trick. It did it for Yassir Arafat. It did it for Saddam Hussein. The point here is that the present wave of mistrust of business and other institutions is not the first in living memory. If it were, it would be more likely to blow over. But mistrust of institutions, especially business, is a recurring phenomenon in American life. The United States is now well launched into the third wave of mistrust of business and other institutions over the past three-quarters of a century.

The first wave occurred in the 1930s. This was the era of the Great Depression, a traumatic event that seared the lives of all who lived through it. Its major symptom was massive un-yielding unemployment affecting an overwhelming one-third of the workforce and indirectly undermining the standard of living of all but the wealthiest Americans.

The consequences of the Great Depression transformed American political and economic life. Herbert Hoover, the Re-publican president who had the bad luck to usher in the De-pression, was summarily dumped, along with the influence and credibility of the Republican Party. Even though the Re-publicans regained the White House in 1953 with Dwight David Eisenhower and again in 1969 with Richard Nixon, the domi-nant political ideology of the nation remained left of center for more than four decades, under the towering shadow of Frank-lin Delano Roosevelt. It wasn't until the election of Ronald Rea-gan in 1980, almost a half-century after the onset of the Great Depression, that the Republicans regained the ideological dominance they had enjoyed in the pre-Depression era, grad-ually succeeding in shifting the nation's political center of grav-ity from left to right of center, where it now resides.

In the chaotic years of the 1930s the mistrust of business was so intense and so widespread that it threatened to topple capitalism itself. Anticapitalist ideologies—Marxist, Trotskyite, socialist—gained a foothold, and in some quarters more than a foothold. Antibusiness ideologies might even have prevailed were it not for the flood of business and social legislation that the Roosevelt administration introduced, against fierce busi-ness opposition. Most business executives and political con-

servatives hated Franklin Roosevelt: they saw him as a traitor
to his upper-class origins. But Roosevelt himself brushed aside
this calumny, insisting that his purpose was fundamentally con-
servative: to save capitalism from its own excesses. The retrospect of history has vindicated Roosevelt's self-description.

The Depression—and the era of mistrust—did not end
until the United States entered World War II after the Japanese
attack on Pearl Harbor on December 7, 1941. From beginning
to end, this wave had persisted for more than a decade.

The second wave of mistrust endured from the late 1960s
to 1980—a roughly equivalent span of years. The source of the
mistrust in those years differed from that of the Great Depression. This was the era of the war in Vietnam and of the Water-
gate scandal and its cover-up, which drove Richard Nixon from
office. These political events converged with serious economic
stagflation (the combined levels of unemployment and infla-
tion exceeded 20 percent). The nation's productivity and com-
petitiveness were so badly stalled that Americans feared that
the Japanese economy would overtake our own.

Unlike the 1930s, when mistrust was sharply focused on
business, virtually all institutions got caught up in the 1970s
wave of mistrust. Gallup tracking polls revealed a precipitous
decline of trust in government. In 1964, before the wave of
mistrust hit, an impressive three-quarters of all Americans believed that "you can trust the federal government to do the
right thing (almost all or most of the time)." By 1980 that hefty
majority had shrunk to a mere one-fourth minority. Tracking
polls conducted by Yankelovich, Skelly and White, Inc., showed
decline of confidence in business to be nearly as extreme,
plunging from 70 percent in 1968 to 29 percent in 1980. Harris
tracking polls revealed a similar pattern for other institutions:
from 1966 to 1982, confidence in the medical profession fell

from 71 percent to 32 percent, in universities from 61 percent to 30 percent, and in the media from a miserably low starting point of 29 percent to less than half of that number (14 percent). So pervasive was this climate of mistrust that it even affected the attitudes of individual Americans toward one another. *Washington Post,* Kaiser, and Harvard University polls showed that in 1968 a majority of Americans (56 percent) believed that "most other people can be trusted." By 1980 even this rudimentary precondition for civil society had suffered. A 39 percent minority had replaced that majority.

The current wave of mistrust in the business sector began to build momentum in 2002. If it follows the same pattern as the other two waves, it is still in its early stages. Most of those who lived through the first wave in the 1930s are retired or deceased. But that is decidedly not the case for those who lived through the second wave of mistrust in the late 1960s and 1970s. They are part of the baby boomer generation—a generation that exercises unprecedented influence on American life. In their formative years, boomers grew up in a pervasive climate of mistrust of business and government authority. The dominant attitude they learned at that time was that business puts its own interests first—ahead of the public's interests or those of its customers and employees.

In the 1980s and 1990s, by virtue of huge effort and success, American business restored its high standing, regaining much of the prestige and trust it had lost in the previous decades. But it is now squandering that trust once again. As it does so, the groundwork of mistrust laid down in earlier years will make it far more difficult to recover the public's trust. When inclinations of mistrust take hold in people's formative years, these are readily reawakened and reinforced, making the new layer of mistrust more difficult to penetrate. I have charted this phenomenon in Figure 2 below, based on survey data with the public.

I believe we should take the new wave of mistrust seriously. Mistrust is a corrosive emotion that distorts everything it touches. The financier Felix Rohatyn offers the cogent observation that "only capitalists can destroy capitalism." His point is that market economies now dominate the world stage; they are too strong and too well ensconced to be destroyed by anticapitalist movements like socialism, communism, or Islamic fundamentalism. But they can be undermined by the actions of those currently in charge—the corporate CEOs, the economic theorists, and the political policy makers who rule capitalist enterprise. The smooth functioning of the market depends on trust. And the surest way to undermine our market economy is by letting mistrust run amok.

It is particularly difficult to lead corporate enterprises in periods of mistrust because the mistrust deprives business leaders of the benefit of the doubt. For example, when Merck's CEO, Raymond Gilmartin, withdrew Vioxx from the market in 2004, he believed that his action would be hailed as a sign of corporate and personal integrity. Instead, he was pilloried for not having taken action sooner. Far from being credited with an act of stewardship, the CEO saw his company's stock plunge 40 percent overnight and found himself at the vortex of a storm of ugly accusations. He resigned before his scheduled retirement. Had these same events taken place in a period of trust and confidence in corporate business, he might have been given the benefit of the doubt and the story might have unfolded in a more benign fashion.

Gilmartin's situation is not unique. CEOs of large corporations are always confronted with confusing cross-pressures and ambiguities. That is the nature of their job. Dealing sure-

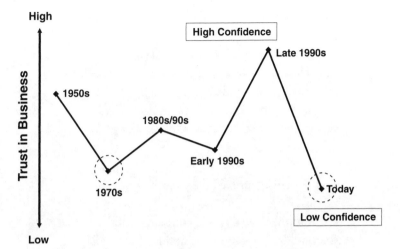

Figure 2. The "screwed again" effect

footedly with these cross-pressures is what CEOs are paid vast sums of money to do. For the most part, the day-to-day management of corporations can be left to others—to so-called COOs (chief operating officers). It is how well CEOs cope with tough ethical and business cross-pressures that separates the successful companies from the unsuccessful. And this is where the ethical norms embodied in a company's corporate culture (and those of the CEO personally) play a critically important role.

Consider, for example, the cross-pressures on CEOs in relation to how they treat employees. These days, many chief executives have strained the bonds of their relationship with employees to the breaking point by transmitting a confusing mixed message. It is not the message they intend to transmit. But it is the message that comes through.

One part of the mixed message is:

> Our corporate vision reveals an exciting path to fu-
> ture success in the new global economy. We know
> the only way it will become a reality is if you, our
> people, buy into it, and give it every ounce of dedi-
> cation and commitment you have to give. Our suc-
> cess depends on you.

The other part of the mixed message is:

> Our number 1 goal in the company is to maximize
> shareholder value. In the pursuit of that goal, you,
> the employee, are expendable. We expect loyalty,
> dedication, and top performance from you, but you
> must understand that you cannot expect loyalty or
> dedication in return.

The reason for the mixed message is that two very different business logics drive today's management. The first goes
something like this:

- We have entered a period of brutal global competition.
- In this environment, our success depends on our
  competitive performance.
- For profitability in today's global marketplace, we
  cannot count as much as in the past on rapid
  growth through expanding markets. We have to be
  strong enough to achieve profitability and growth
  through strengthening our share of market by
  being more competitive.

- Winning a bigger share of market calls for a superior level of customer focus: the name of the game is knowing customers and serving their needs better than the competition.
- The best way to achieve superior customer focus is ensuring that your own people are highly motivated. Employees who are just going through the motions and doing the minimum they have to do to protect their jobs cannot deliver superior customer focus.
- A global marketplace is full of opportunities as well as threats. Through leveraging our core competencies, we have developed a vision of a dynamic, creative, highly profitable organization—but everything depends on implementation: our people have to share our vision and give their utmost in skill, dedication, and commitment.

This business logic says to employees: "You are indispensable to the company's success." But there is a second business logic that leads to the opposite conclusion. It starts the same way: "brutal global competition . . . greater emphasis on performance . . . rich rewards that come only with outstanding profit performance." But then the logic diverges and develops along a different line of thought which goes something like this:

- Success these days is measured in terms of share price, with an ever larger chunk of our compensation coming in the form of bonuses and stock options from which we benefit only if the price of the stock goes up.

- The best way to raise the price of the stock is to ac-
celerate the company's rate of profitability. Companies whose profits grow slowly are penalized by
investor unwillingness to pay a premium on their
earnings; companies whose profits grow at a fast
rate often earn a substantial premium.
- Greatly improved profitability in this environment can be achieved only one way: by cutting
costs to the bone.
- There are many bad features of the new global
economy, but one of its good features is that a
large corporation can call upon a global labor
force—and not just for unskilled labor: you can
get top-notch Russian scientists for $100 a month,
and top-notch Indian programmers for $130 a
week. There is a huge pool of highly motivated,
low-cost labor available in other countries, if one
is willing to think globally.
- For this and other reasons, the domestic labor
market is weak and likely to remain so. The unions
have lost much of their clout, and with the down-
sizing of middle management, there are plenty of
good people available on a part-time or freelance
basis to whom we don't need to give benefits or
raises.
- We can reduce our labor costs to a minimum,
with wondrous impact on our profit margins,
share prices, and stock options.

This logic leads to the second message that employees
hear: "You are dispensable."

Companies that follow this logic do not typically adopt a hostile or adversarial stance toward their employees. Rather, their attitude is a wholly impersonal one, reflecting their conviction that labor costs are a function of the market. You manage people the same way you manage money.

But of course, employees are not the same as plant and equipment and other capital expenditures. People react; machines do not. Moreover, people react differently than expected. When they feel expendable or exploited, they react by holding back as much of themselves as they can without risking their jobs. They may sell their time and raw labor for money, but not their dedication, loyalty, and commitment.

Research conducted by DYG SCAN (a trend-tracking service for corporate clients) shows five patterns of contemporary employee response:

1. Employees no longer believe that their jobs will be secure even if they perform well.
2. They no longer believe in employer loyalty and concern, and consequently lack personal commitment. (Only about one in five corporate employees shows strong commitment.)
3. Many employees have lost confidence that they will be rewarded for learning and expanding their skills. They are beginning to suspect that expertise gained through effort and experience on the job is no longer seen by employers as *valuable* but as making one a more expensive employee.
4. There is even growing skepticism about the corporate emphasis on quality. In quality enhancement programs, improved quality is equated

with fewer, not more, employees, resulting in a *devaluation* of employees by the corporation.

5. Other than the money that can be earned, work in large corporations has become a less reliable source of satisfaction.[1]

Today's corporate trumpet emits an uncertain sound. The mixed message that leaves employees confused, mistrustful, and fearful of the future is a symptom of a larger problem of ethical failure in leadership—the loss of a moral compass. These business executives are having a difficult time reconciling the norms they bring to their own personal and family relationships with corporate norms and pressures to exceed last quarter's earnings.

III
*Un*enlightened Self-Interest

The current climate of mistrust poisons the atmosphere. It tempts observers to grow judgmental and to blame the ethical scandals on an all-encompassing "culture of corruption." The tendency to resort to punitive legalism creates a mood in which it seems natural to hold jury trials in which highly visible CEOs (yesterday's culture heroes) face the kind of stiff prison sentences that one ordinarily associates with rape and armed robbery.

L. Dennis Kozlowski, the former CEO of Tyco, a giant conglomerate with 270,000 employees and $36 billion in annual sales, is believed to have stolen $170 million from the company. He is also accused of hiding unauthorized bonuses to himself and his chief financial officer, lending himself money from the company and then forgiving the loans so that they didn't have to be repaid, and lying to the public about the company's finances in order to pump up the price of the stock. Charged with grand larceny, falsifying business records, conspiracy, and business law violations, he has received a long prison sentence.

Bernard Ebbers, former CEO of WorldCom, has been convicted of pulling off an $11 billion fraud leading to the largest bankruptcy in American history, with employees and investors as the main victims. The charges against him include conspiracy, fraud, and filing false reports. He received a twenty-five-year prison term.

Richard Scrushy, former CEO of HealthSouth, was accused of "orchestrating a huge accounting fraud," an accusation supported by no fewer than five former CFOs at the company. He was tried in his hometown of Birmingham, Alabama, the beneficiary of much HealthSouth largesse. He was acquitted. Kenneth Lay, the former CEO of Enron is accused of the same fraud on a grander scale. He faces court trial.

Criminal indictments and long prison sentences against former culture heroes may satisfy the public's craving for justice, but they are unlikely to raise the level of business ethics. Legalistic solutions and jail terms are not enough to lead to positive initiatives. A backlash is already setting in, with business groups claiming that excessive regulation is counterproductive, producing "unintended consequences that are having significant negative effects on our economy."[1]

My argument is that instead of a primarily legalistic framework, we should adopt a primarily normative one. We should view the scandals as signs of a weakened system of ethical norms that happens to be particularly severe in the business world, but which is not confined to business. Taking strong legal action against those who wantonly break the law can reinforce ethical norms. But it cannot substitute for them.

One reason for the decline of corporate ethical norms is that the temptations are so huge. But other reasons are more compelling, such as the phenomenon that the psychologist Irving Janis terms *groupthink*. Groupthink is the tendency of people who live and work in isolated subcultures to develop distorted views of the world because they talk mainly with one another, cutting themselves off from the viewpoints of others. In such isolation, misconceptions go unchallenged, blind spots go unnoticed, and wishful thinking hardens into received wisdom.

Groupthink is not confined to the business world. It thrives virtually everywhere, even (or especially) in places like universities that pride themselves on their independent thinking. But the pressures of groupthink in corporate life are particularly powerful. (This is one reason that the concept of "corporate culture" has so much resonance in the business world: its inhabitants are all too familiar with its workings.)

Groupthink forces people toward uniformity of norms, often at the expense of their own personal values. We are all familiar with the seeming paradox of executives who are warm and generous with their families and friends while behaving like cutthroats in the workplace. They live in two different universes of values—observing the cultural norms associated with loving families and close bonds at home, then adopting the norms associated with competitive success in the marketplace. Nor do they feel torn between these conflicting values, since they see each as appropriate for its particular settings and activities.

In other words, once a set of norms takes hold in the corporate world, groupthink ensures that it will become widespread and influential. If the norms are unethical (as seen through the lens of the larger society), they can nonetheless exercise a compelling influence on people who see themselves as highly ethical. This robs society of its two most powerful constraints on keeping average law-abiding people on a straight and narrow path: *shame* and *guilt.* Shame and guilt are the powerful mechanisms that enforce social norms—shame is imposed by one's fellows, while guilt is the distress that arises from violating an internalized code of conduct. As corporate norms have shifted to condone behaviors that were once deemed unacceptable, the kinds of behavior that would inspire shame and guilt have likewise shifted. Yesterday's executive might have suffered guilt from cooking the books; today's might feel shame at showing insufficient tough-mindedness in a business deal.

Which current business norms lead an executive to commit outrageously unethical acts while continuing to maintain a self-image free of shame or guilt? If we understand what these destructive norms are and why they exert such a strong influence on our culture, we will have taken the first step toward stopping the scandals; we will have identified the norms that have to change.

Destructive Norms

It may be useful to clarify what we mean by destructive norms. The concept sounds odd, almost oxymoronic. Norms are positive values. They are the unwritten rules that make communal living possible. As such, they form an inherent part of every society's culture. They represent the forms of behavior that are acceptable or unacceptable in each of the roles people occupy in a society: husband, wife, father, mother, child, parent, neighbor, relative, tribal chief, warrior, employee, citizen, consumer, rich man, mendicant, and so on. In some traditional societies, norms are rigidly, even brutally, enforced (for example, stoning a woman charged with adultery). In our own society, most norms have grown more flexible (for example, the widespread acceptance of unmarried couples living together).

Because norms dictate socially desirable behavior, it may at first glance be confusing to speak of *destructive* norms (undesirable behavior). But an instant's thought should clarify the confusion. From the point of view of our culture, stoning women—for any reason—is totally unacceptable; in some fundamentalist societies, it is unacceptable *not* to severely punish women accused of adultery. Clearly, norms vary from culture to culture. Within any culture, we also find wide variations in norms from subculture to subculture—a major source of tension between religious conservatives and other subcultures in our own society. Also, norms often conflict and pull individuals in different directions: the norms governing competition conflict with the norms prescribing cooperative and considerate behavior; the norms of self-expression collide with norms of civility.

A series of conflicting norms of ethical behavior has plunged our society into a state of confusion and disorientation. This is what people mean when they say we have lost our moral compass. They are not saying that the culture has grown evil and mean-spirited (some may believe this, but not the majority). What concerns the majority of Americans today is the suspicion that our traditional norms of right and wrong are being blurred, leaving people confused and easily tempted to go down the wrong path. The corporate scandals that do not involve outright criminality do involve cutting corners, bending the rules, gaming the system, ignoring conflicts of interest, putting one's own interests ahead of others, and seeking to win at any cost. Those guilty of such behaviors do not see themselves as bad people violating society's norms; they see themselves as bold, venturesome, innovative, smart people who are living by the norms of contemporary corporate life and who deserve to reap the rewards for doing so.

It is in this sense that norms may be destructive. From the perspective both of the culture and the individual corpo-

ration, some of the newer norms are dysfunctional and destructive. This phenomenon of conflicting norms was clearly
on display in the experience of our troops in Iraq. The official
norms of the military dictate that prisoner abuse is unacceptable; at the same time a normative climate that encouraged
prisoner abuse had clearly been established, with the two sets
of norms in confusing conflict with each other.

Seven Deadly Norms

It would be wrong to imply that destructive norms have taken
over the business community. This is emphatically not the
case. Unfortunately, there is no reliable way to quantify just
how far ethically pernicious norms have spread. The truth lies
somewhere between "a few bad apples" and "a culture of corruption." The scope, magnitude, and frequency of the scandals
do imply that something systemic is wrong. In 2004 the Corporate Fraud Task Force of the Justice Department charged
more than nine hundred executives with fraud and obtained
more than five hundred corporate fraud convictions. The SEC
filed more than six hundred civil enforcement actions involving fraud.[2] This is certainly more than a few bad apples, especially when one realizes that it represents a minuscule fraction
of corporate wrongdoing.

On the other hand, there is strong evidence that the taint
has not spread throughout business. In many companies, the
dominant norm remains the smell test—the conviction that
staying within the letter of the law is not good enough and that
the company must adhere to ethical standards of right and
wrong that go beyond the law. Yet in recent years, a number of
dysfunctional norms have crept into the culture, aided and
abetted by groupthink. Seven destructive norms converge with

one another to form an *über*-norm that might well be called *un*enlightened self-interest.

I will elaborate on these in later chapters, but here briefly are the seven deadly norms that are causing most of ethical confusion in the nation, particularly in the business community:

1. EQUATING WRONGDOING EXCLUSIVELY WITH ILLEGALITY

To the extent that shame and guilt still operate in our society and are linked to wrongdoing, and to the extent that wrongdoing is linked solely to breaking the law, then one is off the hook simply by staying within the letter of the law. As noted earlier, there is no more corrosive deterioration in today's ethical norms than the conviction that "I didn't do anything illegal, so I didn't do anything wrong."

2. WIN AT ANY COST

The norm that winning is all that matters and that everything else is unimportant pervades the larger society but becomes particularly consequential in corporate settings. Since competition is a dominant theme in business, it reinforces the aggressive urge to win without fussing too much about the tactics for doing so. Corporations often deploy their resources in a zero-sum form of winning: if we win, you have to lose.

Because we have become such a highly individualistic society, the fierce need to win at all costs readily spreads from the company to the individual. We can see this norm at work in countless small instances in our society, from a driver who cuts another off in order to gain a few yards' advantage on a congested freeway to a parent screaming abuse at the coach when his or her child's soccer team loses a game.

3. GAMING THE SYSTEM IS GOOD SPORT

There are large elements of fun and game-playing in seeing how far one can go gaming the system. Enron was full of computer-savvy young people who spent days and weeks with their complex computer models figuring out how to drive up the price of energy artificially (for example, through deliberately closing refineries for maintenance and repair in California to create the maximum bottleneck).

When the desire to beat the system converges with the imperative to win, the result is a deadly combination, ensuring that the energies of gifted young people will be devoted to activities whose ethical consequences are easily shoved into the background.

4. CONFLICT OF INTEREST IS FOR WIMPS

One of the deadliest norms in business today is the tendency to ignore or brush aside conflicts of interest as lily-livered concerns that should not interfere with making as much money as the traffic will bear. This norm is especially flagrant on Wall Street and in the insurance industry, where playing both sides of a transaction has become an art form. Practitioners protect themselves from shame and guilt by developing bland Orwellian language to describe their double-dealing transactions. The phrase "conflict of interest" is itself bloodless and legalistic. It carries none of the pungency associated with plain-talking phrases like "betraying the customer's trust" or "getting kickbacks for pushing clients into the worst performing funds."

The hypocrisy is obvious to Wall Street's own ethically concerned leaders. The celebrated Wall Street analyst Byron Wien has written extensively about "the breaking of the covenant between corporations and investors."[3] Unfortunately, Wien's concerns have done little to change Wall Street's habits.

5. THE CEO AS ROYALTY

In the 1990s CEOs became celebrities, partly for their outsized paychecks and partly because of the dazzling performance of the stock market in the years leading up to the bursting of the bubble. Little need be said here about the corrupting influence of money, power, and adulation. It has all been said before. Power goes to people's heads. Few can handle it well. The usual response is arrogance and the conviction that your whims should be instantly indulged, no questions asked. There is no other explanation for the excesses of people like Kozlowski, the Rigas family, Lord Black, Kenneth Lay, Bernie Ebbers, Franklin Raines, and countless others.

The destructive norm here is the assumption that the power and grandeur of the CEO is so great that he (and sometimes she) is exempt from the norms that ordinary mortals are forced to observe.

6. TWISTING THE CONCEPT OF SHAREHOLDER VALUE

This deadly norm is specific to business, which I discuss at length in Chapter 8. The rationale usually given for putting shareholders first is that by serving the long-term interests of committed investors, the company also serves the interests of its other stakeholders—employees, customers, suppliers, local

community, the society at large. In practice, however, shareholder value does not live up to its rationale because it suffers
from two crippling distortions. The more obvious distortion is
the emphasis on short-term quarterly earnings reports—the
ones that clever accountants can most easily manipulate. The
less obvious but arguably more serious distortion relates to the
identity of the so-called "owners." The phrase conjures up im-
ages of Warren Buffet–type investors who buy and hold their
stock for the long haul, or of Grandpa in Cleveland whose retirement is made comfortable by the dividends the stock pays.
In practice, shareholder value has little to do with committed
investors and owners of the company's shares, and everything
to do with thirty-year-old mutual fund managers with zero
loyalty to the company who can and do dump the stock without a second's hesitation. They are short-term renters of the
stock, not committed owners. In both cases, there is a destructive shift from a long-term to a short-term focus.

In combination, these distortions make a mockery of
shareholder value's stated intention of aligning the interests
of management more closely with those of the company's
"owners."

7. FREE-MARKET ECONOMIES REQUIRE DEREGULATION

This is perhaps the subtlest of the seven deadly norms—and
some scholars believe it is the deadliest.[4] It ties into the laissez-
faire strain of the capitalist tradition. Executives hold highly
abstract and theoretical assumptions about the nature of corporations and market economies. One such assumption is the
image of the corporation as an impersonal machine. Driven by

inexorable laws of profit maximization, these corporate machines cannot afford constraints like regulation or sentimentality about people's feelings and lives. This notion that the corporation runs according to inescapable, impersonal, and rigid economic laws has fostered a great deal of ill-advised deregulation, as well as rigidity, inflexibility, and undue suffering.

The experience of many nations, especially our own, has demonstrated that a market economy is not a machine with a fixed inherent nature but a system that can be remarkably flexible. The position of CEO in a large multinational corporation is the pressure point in the system. It is where all the conflicting and contradictory pressures of the modern global economy converge. This makes the job of the CEO immensely complicated. But it also makes it compelling and important. CEOs are the change agents of the emerging global economy.

A free-market economy is not well served by the automaton CEO who identifies totally with the notion of a market-driven enterprise as a machine that cannot, and should not, be constrained by regulation. It is well served by the very human CEO who brings his or her own well-developed ethical values into the job and calls upon these for guidance in juggling corporate cross-pressures.

In subsequent chapters we will return in one way or another to each of these seven deadly norms. For present purposes, however, I would underscore a single point. The combined effect of these seven norms is undermining traditional American adherence to the principle of enlightened self-interest—the notion that one can do well by doing good. Compositely, they lead instead to *un*enlightened self-interest—that one should do well at all costs and forget about doing good. Admittedly, enlightened self-interest is a tough guide to follow: it requires a conscious effort to integrate personal advantage and larger social benefits. But unenlightened self-interest is a disaster for institutions that are meant to serve the needs of the larger community.

IV
Yesterday's versus Today's Ethical Norms

These seven deadly norms can be grouped into two broad categories—norms that come from within the business community and norms rooted in the general culture. The business norms are the "shareholders-come-first" norm that focuses on who the main beneficiaries of corporate success should be, and the "let-business-be-business" norm that leads to deregulation.

The shareholders-come-first norm derives from a shift in corporate culture that is only a few decades old. The norm that the laws of the free market brook no interference, intervention, or regulation is much older. It derives from economic theories that go all the way back to Adam Smith. The premise here is that if you monkey with the iron laws of market capitalism, be it through government regulation or capricious management practices (such as selling below cost, or being overly generous to employees), you will ruin the enterprise. There is certainly some validity to this observation, but it is subject to distortion and overstatement.

These two norms are rooted in the belief systems of the business community and have little to do with the general culture. The other five norms, however, flow directly from the culture at large. All five originate in social trends that exploded on the national scene in the 1960s and 1970s. Our culture has been struggling ever since to reconcile these new norms with more traditional ones. For ease of reference, I call the five social norms "winning-for-myself" norms.

In this chapter, I take a brief backward glance at the origin of the winning-for-myself norms that have migrated from the culture at large to the business community. In later chapters, I will dig into the sources of the shareholders-come-first and the deregulatory norms—the norms directly linked to business.

Winning for Myself

The five norms that make up the winning-for-myself set of norms push individualistic values toward an extreme focus on one's own needs, desires, and interests. They directly challenge our more traditional ethos of sacrifice and concern for others. To the men and women who compete vigorously with one another in today's corporations, it whispers this message:

> If you really want it and it's not illegal, go for it. If you want to win—and winning is important in a society that can be cruel and unforgiving to losers—you may have to bend the rules. Trying to avoid conflicts of interest is for wimps. Besides, gaming the system is a fun sport: it's a challenge to pit your brains and skills against others. Winning through gaming the system not only brings you the material

rewards you deserve, it proves that you are smart and a survivor. Moreover, the closer you get to the top, the less the rules apply to you. If you become CEO, you call the shots.

This ethic derives from the transformation in values that took place in our culture from the mid-sixties to the eighties. Before then, a different set of ethical norms prevailed. Norms and ethics are not as a rule written down formally, so it can be difficult to point to a neatly codified before-and-after picture. However, thanks to an unpublished study, we have a fascinating and revealing window on this comparison.

In the mid-1990s, the *Harvard Business Review* and the Harvard Business School Alumni Office invited me to conduct a series of interviews of the Business School class of 1949—perhaps the most successful graduating class in the B-school's history.[1] The interviews are particularly valuable for our present purposes, because they provide a glimpse of a generation of highly successful business leaders and the norms that guided their actions.

Approximately forty-five years after graduating from the Business School, when most members of this famous class had already retired, we asked them to look back and reflect on their lives and careers, drawing them out about how they had balanced careers with family and other commitments, what they saw as their greatest accomplishments, and how their ethical values and outlook had changed over the forty-five years since they had graduated.

Strikingly, one of the first findings to surface from the interviews was a powerful set of ethical principles. Most class members credited their parents with instilling in them strong principles that they said had guided them throughout their

lives. The men—and all graduates in the 1940s were male—
said they were brought up in a manner in which obligation
and responsibility were as automatic to them as breathing.
They took it for granted that responsibility requires hard
work, sacrifice, independence, and taking care of others.

When asked what they saw as their most important business norms, a whopping 97 percent identified "personal integrity—being straight with people and avoiding the quick
buck if it means cutting corners." The second most important
norm (96 percent) was "giving your customers or clients full
value for the money." One respondent summed it up this way:
"My father and I were partners for thirty-five years. [He
stressed] doing things right: don't try to knock anyone down,
and money is not the most important thing."

Many members of the class stated that they had often
been under pressure to cut corners. A few admitted that they
had sometimes done so, but now in retrospect they expressed
genuine regret, even though they had gotten away with it at the
time. What is striking is how many said they refused to cut
corners, not because they were afraid of getting caught but because it simply seemed wrong:

- "There comes a time when the organization demands that you do something and there's no way
  you can do this and still live with yourself. I was
  the vice president of the organization, and it demanded that I do certain things that I considered
  not appropriate, and I walked out. I walked away."
- "I used to have falling outs . . . because I would
  not bend my ethics to fit the situation, and I find
  that in business it is inevitable to find people for
  whom results come first and ethics come second

instead of the other way around. . . . I did not always endear myself to my boss."

Sometimes, the interviewees admitted, playing the game was more important than meeting the goals of the business. This is not to say they didn't want to win. Most enjoyed the excitement and challenge of being players. As one said: "To me business has been a chess game, and when you play the chess game well and you win that's very exciting. I used to be accused of being more anxious to do a difficult deal that was less remunerative than a simple deal that was more remunerative."

While the thrill of winning and coming out on top—of being number one—was a powerful motivator for these men, the satisfaction of passing on what they had learned and giving back to the larger society loomed just as large. The class of 1949 showed a powerful service ethic. When asked what they considered their greatest accomplishment in their careers, the top response was helping other people and other companies succeed. They also placed giving back to the community near the top of the list, far above getting public recognition, setting a company record, or being promoted. One respondent put it this way: "My mother taught us a sense of noblesse oblige—that we had to give something back. She wanted us to be successful, but she also wanted us to be successful in the sense that we would be serving society."

Almost every member of the class was deeply involved in community activity of one sort or another, much of it arising from a deeply held need to give something back to the community, to help those who need help, to answer a religious call to service, and to adhere to strong ethical standards.

Many members of the class observed that today's newly minted MBAs had a shakier ethical compass than their own.

When asked what the school should be teaching its students today, "ethics" was the far and away the top response (54 percent, outstripping other responses by a ratio of 3 to 1). And the class's advice for new B-school grads followed a similar pattern. Among the top-rated pieces of advice "strongly urged" by more than 70 percent of respondents, three relate to ethics:

- Put the ethical side ahead of everything else; character is more important than skills (83 percent)
- Always remember that family is more important than your career (72 percent)
- Make time for community service (71 percent)

In their stories, respondents provided compelling descriptions what it meant to act ethically:

- "Telling the truth. Being square. Caring about the people that work for you. Having a real loyalty down as well as expecting loyalty up."
- "I think it started when I was a choirboy in Manhattan. I didn't like it and my parents said, 'You joined. You have a job to do and you're going to that church every Sunday and sing in that choir. ... You've got a responsibility.' ... They laid down the law: 'When you make a promise to do something, you do it.' That was a big influence."
- "Integrity and honesty by example. A harder worker there never was than my foster father. He was a grocer—honest and reliable. If he made a mistake on a bill he'd give the money back."

These more traditional norms can be encapsulated as follows:

> Work hard. Live by the rules. Follow a firm set of ethical principles that distinguishes right from wrong. Show respect for the rights of others. Practice self-discipline ("You can't have everything you want when you want it"). Realize that self-respect is more important than winning, and that being a leader means putting the needs of others ahead of your own.

What I find most striking in the comparison between past and present is how strongly members of the class of 1949 had been influenced by their parents, and how active those parents had been at drumming ethical principles into their children. This pattern did not repeat itself in the next generation: class of '49ers appeared much more reluctant to impose their own inherited ethical values on their children. Those children and others of the same era—the baby boom generation—were left to invent their own ethical standards.

In many ways, boomer ethical standards are an improvement over the often narrow, bigoted, conformist views of their fathers. But in one fateful way, they are a step backward: the ethic of winning for others as well as for yourself gave way, all too often, to a more narcissistic focus on the self.

A Cultural Revolution

The transformation from the class of 1949 era to the current era confronts us with one of the sharpest discontinuities of values in our history as a culture. I have had the good fortune to track our nation's "cultural revolution" (for that is what it has proven to be) over the past forty years. In the early 1960s, my public opinion survey firm, Yankelovich, Skelly and White, identified a "forerunner" group of college students who had begun to question some of their parents' core values. These young people had concluded that their fathers' nose-to-the-grindstone way of life and their mothers' sacrifice of self for the family somehow didn't make sense in a time of growing affluence. They felt that sacrifice for the family was acceptable if you were obliged to do it. But if it proved economically un-necessary, why sacrifice something as important as one's own self-expressive needs?[2]

In the mid-1960s we launched a series of annual studies on the great transformations in social values occurring among our nation's young people. So far-reaching were the shifts in values that we decided to monitor them on a regular basis, and ever since 1969 we have conducted an annual survey of chang-ing American social values.[3]

By the end of the 1970s we had documented the fact that the student "forerunner" attitudes of the sixties had spread rapidly beyond the nation's campuses—from 3 percent of the population in the mid-sixties (the college-attending chil-dren of affluent, well-educated parents) to 80 percent of adult Americans by the late seventies! To be sure, the dispersion was not universal, and among the 80 percent, a majority was highly selective in picking and choosing among the new values they found most congenial. But nonetheless it was an extraordinary transformation in social values of the sort that one usually as-sociates with generations or even centuries.[4]

Our tracking data suggest that societies learn and react differently than do individuals. Surprisingly, social learning is often far more abrupt than individual learning. It is more extreme, less incremental. Individuals who encounter new circumstances will usually adjust to them in a slow and moderate fashion. They have learned that cautious adjustments keep them from making bad mistakes. But for a variety of reasons, societies react far less cautiously. They tend to lurch abruptly from one extreme to the other.

Our research labeled this pattern of sudden swings to the opposite extreme, followed by gradual adaptations, "lurch and learn." A typical lurch-and-learn pattern starts with a sharp lurch in norms, followed by complex (and much more gradual) modifications based on trial-and-error experimentation. Some of these experiments inevitably go awry. People do not always draw the right lessons from trial-and-error learning.

Consider the goal of self-fulfillment. In the sixties and seventies the assumption prevailed that self-fulfillment consisted of filling as many personal needs as possible: the more needs you satisfy, the more self-fulfilled you become. This is the ethos of "you can have it all"—career, family, affluence, leisure, self-esteem, sexual gratification, self-expression, and guaranteed entitlements. In the moral domain, the norms of the fifties lurched all the way from automatic sacrifice for others to: "If I want it and it isn't illegal, why shouldn't I have it?" This lurch from sacrifice for others (the prevailing norm of the fifties) to "meet my every need" (the prevailing norm of the sixties and seventies) has not proven as satisfying and successful as baby boomers had assumed it would be.

In the society at large (if not yet in the business community), a shift is now occurring toward a perception of the self as a moral actor with obligations as well as rights. There is a growing realization that lots of perfectly legal actions hurt other people and are ethically wrong. The ancient truth that moral imperatives generally collide with individual desires and that there is such a thing as "right" and "wrong" is regaining favor. In our tracking studies, we are beginning to measure a shift back toward absolute as distinct from relative values. This is not to say that Americans want to return to some nostalgic vision of the glory days of the 1950s—as a nation we have made enormous gains in diversity, tolerance, and inclusiveness since then that few Americans would be willing to reverse. But the nation is retreating from the extremes of relativism to a more universal code of standards and behaviors.[5]

A trend toward social Darwinism also shows up clearly in our recent tracking data. It reveals a shift away from the kind of egalitarianism dominant in the 1960s and 1970s, which dictated that everyone was entitled to share in the bounty of available resources, even if this required large-scale redistribution. The assumption then was that unequal results were society's fault, and that it was society's obligation to address and correct them. We are now moving back toward the traditional American norm that people are responsible for their own lives, and that the reality of life is such that there inevitably will be both winners and losers. This conception limits the society's moral and legal obligations, but it does not rule out compassion. The prevailing view today is compassion "yes," legal obligation "no." Unequal results are no longer deemed to be society's fault.

In sum, the picture I derive from four decades of annual tracking studies of America's changing social trends is that our society currently finds itself in an unstable place, ethically speaking. The extreme hedonism, narcissism, insistence on having it all, and moral relativism of the postsixties era have passed, as has the assumption that economic affluence has become the permanent condition of American life. These have been moderated by the long process of learning, consolidation, and adaptation that followed on the initial lurch. Divorce, for instance, was socially taboo in the 1950s, then "lurched" into being considered a reasonable, even desirable means for adults to express their individual needs, regardless of its impact on the other spouse and children. Under the pressure of a long period of trial and experimentation, that extreme position has now moderated to a more nuanced view: most people feel that divorce is acceptable (if regrettable), but that it should be considered a last resort when there are young children involved.

Today, Americans are painfully and awkwardly struggling with ethical issues in their individual and family lives, moving back from the precarious edge of relativism toward moral absolutes. In our institutions, however, especially our economic institutions, the struggle is more muted. Business, like any subculture, exists in partial isolation from the larger society. As such it has fewer opportunities to test and adapt its norms—to engage in the "learning" that follows the "lurch." The pressures of groupthink, combined with the rewards of continuing to operate according to its currently degraded norms, have made the business world slower to absorb the changing ethical consciousness of the larger society.

The Comfort Zone Factor

As a society, we are quite comfortable with transactions that involve the legal structure on which corporate governance rests—passing laws, introducing regulations, leveling fines and criminal charges against those who break the law, and even eventually tossing them in prison, however high and mighty they may once have been. Our legal mechanisms are well developed. We have the institutions we need to execute these tasks, the apparatus for implementation is in place, we understand at least some of the benefits and drawbacks of our legal system, and we are well endowed with committed professionals to do what needs to be done.

When it comes to reversing the effects of destructive norms, however, we have left our comfort zone far behind. We don't ordinarily think in terms of norms, we don't make sharp, clear distinctions between norms and laws, and we don't have institutions whose main task it is to change norms when they need changing. One reason we look to religion for this indispensable societal obligation is our lack of appropriate secular institutions; but policing norms is a controversial task for religious institutions to undertake, one that can get them and the rest of society into trouble. Sometimes we look to our political leaders for guidance on ethical norms, because politics and ethical norms are deeply intertwined. But here, too, there are serious jurisdictional problems. Political leadership has the right of entry when solutions call for legal action. But it has a less clear-cut mandate when it comes to ethical norms.

In practice this means that our society has to gain enough comfort with the idea of norms to be able to make the changes necessary to our future well being. If we are to add norm changing to our repertoire of cultural skills and capabilities, we ought to have at least a rudimentary understanding of where particular norms come from and what is involved in changing them.

V

Two Incomplete Visions

L et us assume that a coercive legalistic approach is *not* a sufficient solution to the ethical scandals that are tainting business and other institutions—the accounting scandals, the rip-offs, the blatant conflicts of interest, the tainted Wall Street advice, the rigged bids, the cover-ups, the dispiriting picture of the most respected institutions in the land routinely violating the public trust.

What, then, *would be* sufficient?

As is often the case, the solution develops out of how one defines the problem. I have framed the problem as one of weakened ethical norms *and* regulations. And I have suggested that neither legal solutions by themselves nor the status quo in ethical standards will be enough to repair those norms and restore public trust in the integrity of business. We need to advance to a higher level of ethical commitment—the level of stewardship ethics.

One impetus for moving toward stewardship ethics should be public insistence on the difference between law and ethical right and wrong. Average Americans fully realize that someone can stay out of jail and still be guilty of unethical behavior. The broker who steers you to a corrupt mutual fund because the fund is paying him to do so may not be breaking the law, but he (or she) is certainly breaking the unwritten contract of trust between you. Even if that broker agrees to stop accepting so-called "revenue sharing" payoffs, he is unlikely to regain your trust. You will want to find a broker who has a proven commitment to placing your interests ahead of maximizing his own short-term profits. There are such brokers and they are far from poverty stricken. They are successful precisely because they see the business wisdom (as well as the ethical virtue) of subordinating their short-term profits to your—and their own—longer-term interests.

Many years ago I had the good fortune of working with the CEO of the Prudential Life Assurance Company, a man named Orville Beal. What I remember most vividly about Mr. Beal was his commitment to life insurance as "a sacred trust." His management of the Pru's life insurance business was the living embodiment of the stewardship ethic, as conveyed through the old-fashioned term *sacred trust*. Strikingly, the words one hears from marketing executives of the same company today illustrate the shift in ethical outlook between then and now. Instead of words like *sacred trust*, today's Prudential executives speculate on the various ways they can "leverage the Rock" (the Rock of Gibraltar being the longtime symbol of the Pru).

The language of sacred trust sounds quaint in today's go-go economy. But the language of "leveraging the Rock," with its overtones of manipulation and gaming the system, says worlds about what is happening to the moral climate.

How should a complex society such as ours go about revitalizing and upgrading its ethical norms?

A good vantage point for addressing this question is to tune into a societal conversation that has engaged some of our most provocative public intellectuals for the past few decades. The conversation is about what vision of America most deserves our attention and fealty.

As reported in the last chapter of my book *The Magic of Dialogue,* two quite different visions of America have dominated. One is the "vision of the free market." This vision holds that in the new global economy, the free market, driven by technology and entrepreneurship, will shape a more prosperous, democratic and secure world.

The other is the "vision of civil society." This vision sets out to renew America's dream of creating a better and more just society by strengthening some of our most cherished social values: community, faith, responsibility, civic virtue, neighborliness, and mutual concern. The vision of civil society holds that these values are not inherent in market economies. (My use of the term "civil society" is somewhat unconventional: I will explain it further below.)

I have subsequently come to the conclusion that each of these visions is radically incomplete, but that each offers a piece of the solution to our badly tattered institutional ethics.

The Vision of the Free Market

This school of thought holds that to achieve a just society we should let the market work its magic. It posits a free market that is not only a supremely efficient allocator of resources but also a source of ethical strength.

The vision of the free market has been on the ascendancy in the past few decades, both during the economic boom of the nineties and in a somewhat more subdued form in the current

decade. The most utopian form of this vision appeared a number of years ago in a widely-read *Wired* magazine article, "The
Long Boom." In glowing terms, the article conveyed the ideal-
ism as well as the material promise of the free-market vision:

> We are watching the beginnings of a global eco-
> nomic boom on a scale never experienced before . . .
> the early waves of a 25 year run of a greatly ex-
> panding economy that will do much to solve seem-
> ingly intractable problems like poverty and to ease
> tensions throughout the world. . . .
>
> When an economy booms, money courses
> throughout the society, people get rich quick, and
> almost everyone sees an opportunity to improve
> their station in life. . . .
>
> A spirit of generosity returns. The vast major-
> ity of Americans who see their prosperity rising
> with the expanding economy are genuinely sympa-
> thetic to the plight of those left behind. . . .
>
> [The] influx of immigrants . . . brings a pleas-
> ant surprise: the revival of the family. . . . A boom-
> ing economy eases tensions among various ethnic
> and interest groups.
>
> A dramatic reduction in the number of un-
> skilled jobs makes clear that good education is a
> matter of survival. . . . The booming economy pro-
> vides the resources to overhaul education. The
> products of that revamped education system enter
> the economy and improve its productivity. . . .
>
> We're forming a new civilization, a global civ-
> ilization, distinct from those that arose on the
> planet before.[1]

This seemed a credible vision when it first appeared in the heady days of the dotcom bubble. It captured the market's power to transform societies by spurring innovation, creativity, and better living standards. But it also assumed that the free market has moral virtues over and above its ability to allocate resources efficiently. The free market described here not only creates greater wealth, it also furthers the American Dream. It fosters individualism, democracy, generosity, freedom, choice, openness, self-discipline, and responsibility. These moral virtues give the vision of the free market its ideological and political appeal.

The Vision of Civil Society

The vision of civil society is a counterbalance to the vision of the free market. In this work I depart from the conventional use of the term *civil society*. In the political science literature, *civil society* is generally used in a neutral sense, free of implied moral values. *Civil society* in that sense refers descriptively to the nongovernmental parts of society—business, the professions, trade unions, religious institutions, voluntary associations (NGOs), the family, and so on. University of California, San Diego, Professor Sanford Lakoff points out that Hegel, who first used the term, did not include the family, but that Marx and those who followed did.[2] Here, as in later chapters, I endow the concept of *civil society* with a definite set of moral values, because that is the way the vision is often understood in nonacademic contexts. This vision, then, defines civil society as the realm of family, friends, neighbors, schools, churches, and workplaces. It is the home of an ethic different from either the self-interest of the market economy or the coercive force of government. Its ethic reflects voluntary ties of obligation, embodying such values as reciprocity, respect, trust, stability, neighborliness, civic involvement, and love. These values are not inherent in a free-market economy and are in some ways antithetical to it.

Like the concept of free markets, civil society can be used either neutrally or in a value-laden fashion. Each generation endows its market economy with the values and qualities that are important to its society and historical era. In our era, it is especially important that we give attention to the values of civil society as well as to those we attribute to market economies.

The Limits of Each Vision

Each of these visions captures important aspects of our heritage and prospects. But each also contains serious flaws that limit its value as a vision to assist us en route to a stewardship ethics society.

The vision of the free market lays heavy emphasis on the "creative" side of capitalism's capacity for "creative destruction" but neglects its "destructive" aspect. In many ways, a market economy acts like an uncontrollable force of nature: impersonal, implacable, and in the short run radically disruptive of jobs, skills, and older enterprises. For those who succeed in riding the tiger, the capitalism of the free market is wonderful. But it holds less appeal for those who fall in the path of its creative destruction—those whose jobs are outsourced or whose savings are wiped out when their company's stock collapses. The "collateral damage" of market economies can too often be measured in communities uprooted and livelihoods destroyed.

More subtly, free-market visionaries attribute ethical virtues to the market that it does not, in fact, possess. The virtues they emphasize—individualism, freedom, democracy, choice, flexibility, creativity, openness, adaptability, self-improvement, self-discipline, leadership, and responsibility—are in fact *not* inherent in the operations of market economies. Some executives, companies, and governments that wield market power use this mechanism wisely and compassionately. Others use their raw economic power mindlessly and couldn't care less about its destructive fallout.

In *The Magic of Dialogue* I worried about what would happen if the vision of the free market became the sole guiding principle of our society:

> The Vision of the Free Market is a powerful ideology. If it comes to monopolize our culture, it will inexorably undermine the values of civil society. Concepts such as profit maximization, short-term profitability, reliance on part-time temporary workers, shareholder value, downsizing, the accelerating tempo of competition and the ever-widening gap between well-educated, well-paid elites and the majority of the workforce will prevail. Ultimately, Oscar Wilde's description of the cynic who "knows the price of everything and the value of nothing" will come to describe our market-driven culture.[3]

The vision of the free market appeals to the hyperindividualism that is the heritage of recent past. It undercuts the traditional value of "enlightened self-interest"—the notion that in serving their own interests intelligently, farsighted individuals and institutions can also contribute to the interests of the larger community. The ability to unleash the positive power of enlightened self-interest depends on an older, more ethically responsible form of individualism. In contrast, the new hyper-individualism is an expression of the kind of unenlightened self-interest outlined in Chapter 3. When hyperindividualism takes hold, obligations to family and community take a back seat to the drive for self-expression and self-fulfillment, while sacrifice becomes an act of foolishness or even self-betrayal.

Like its counterpart vision of the free market, the vision of civil society has enormous emotional appeal. Most Americans yearn for the values it symbolizes: community, civility, spirituality, and dedication to a higher purpose. But like its counterpart, this vision is also flawed and incomplete.

For one thing, it is based on a nostalgic vision of the past as a kind of civic utopia. Most leaders of the civil society movement are searching to recover something they believe our nation once had and now has lost. They hearken back to Alexis de Tocqueville's classic study in the early part of the nineteenth century, *Democracy in America*. For Tocqueville the most remarkable feature of the United States as it then existed was the richness and vitality of its civil society, by which he meant the proliferation of civic groups, community leaders, and voluntary organizations (firefighters, charities, and so on). Through the principle of "association," he said, these voluntary associations assumed a civic responsibility for the well-being of the society that was absent in the Europe of the time. But it is important not to downplay the long-standing power of self-interest in American life. It is by no means clear that Americans were ever as civically virtuous as we like to remember.

In addition, the vision of civil society has its darker side. In today's America, the connotations of community are all warm and fuzzy. But historically, tight community bonds have also been associated with narrowness, bigotry, xenophobia, mistrust of outsiders, prying eyes, and stultifying social conformity—characteristics not absent from the America of the 1950s. In the past half-century, while the bonds of community may have frayed, America has undergone a revolutionary shift toward becoming a far more pluralistic and socially tolerant nation. Few Americans want to curtail the freedom of choice and individual expression they gained in our own cultural revolution.

The vision of civil society is a source of the ethical values that must complement the creative destruction of our market economy. But it limps along far behind the vision of the free market in vitality, enthusiasm, and power. Some dismiss it as naïve do-gooderism; others are disturbed by the vision of traditional society, intolerant of change and innovation, stifling our exuberant American individualism. As a practical matter, there is no chance that the vision of civil society will prevail over the dynamism of the free-market vision. But the values it embodies are precious to the American people, who would like to see them integrated into the vision of the free market.

In theory, it is easy to draw a sharp distinction between the economic and civil society spheres of our culture. But in practice the two merge and blur into each other. Businesses and other organizations are not just economic institutions. They also bring together people who work side by side every day and who share common interests and a common fate that is dependent on how well the organization functions. In this respect a business is also a community, as is a school, a church, a symphony orchestra, a magazine, a hospital, a branch of science. A company like Procter and Gamble identifies community as one of its core values.

All large corporations have two roles to play at the same time: each serves the practical purpose of providing products and services, but it is also an expression of community and civil society. If it sacrifices the second role, more often than not it will slip into mediocrity or worse. In serving their practical functions, these organizations can to some degree scant their civil society obligation. But as parts of a larger community, they cannot thrive as isolated fragments. They must communicate with one another, understand one another, trust one another, identify with one another. And to do all that they cannot rely exclusively on the values of the marketplace or the entitlements of civil society or the legalisms associated with big government.

In summary, a fog of confusion over ethical norms divides American society and undermines our customary pragmatic, nonideological approach to the problems that beset us, rendering them unsustainable.

While this fog of confusion pervades all of our institutions, its effects are particularly harmful in our corporate community, leading to a series of scandals and deepening a divide of mistrust that disconnects Americans from their institutions.

As a society, we tend to fall back on legalistic solutions and business-as-usual ethics—not because we are confident that these will work, but simply because these are the tools that fit most cozily into our comfort zone. In this work, I have taken the position that you can't fight bad norms solely with laws and regulations. The only way to get rid of the bad norms that currently pervade corporate America is to replace them with norms that are sound both practically and ethically. I acknowledge that our culture is less adept at juggling norms than at juggling legal strategies, but if this is what it takes, we are surely resourceful enough to learn how to do it better.

I have labeled the package of norms that I believe are best for the economy and the society as a whole as *stewardship ethics.* As I shall argue in the following chapters, stewardship ethics offers the ideal way of bridging the gap between the two visions—combining the dynamism and vitality of the free market with the strong ethical grounding of civil society.

I believe the two visions of America provide us with a good point of departure for addressing the all-important issue of practical implementation: how to encourage the norms of stewardship ethics.

Part II
Moving toward
a New Stage of Market
Capitalism through
Stewardship Ethics

VI
Unpacking Stewardship Ethics

W e now turn from framing the problem to finding a solution. The scandals and the mistrust they generate are the problem. Moving toward a new stage of market capitalism through stewardship ethics is the solution.

A full-scale solution requires:

1. A working understanding of what stewardship ethics is and how it differs from corporate social responsibility
2. A vision of how stewardship ethics will affect the business sector
3. A strategy to achieve the vision
4. Tactics to implement the strategy

In this chapter I unpack the concept of stewardship ethics and compare it with corporate social responsibility. In Chapter 7 I elaborate the vision, and in Chapters 8–10 I spell out the strategy and tactics needed to achieve the vision.

Laissez-faire

The core elements of stewardship ethics come into sharpest relief when we compare them with other ways of thinking about the role of ethics in market economies. At present, there are two dominant ways of thinking about ethics in business—the laissez-faire tradition and the corporate social responsibility movement.

Most managers are educated in the laissez-faire tradition to believe that making a company profitable is in itself an ethical good. From a laissez-faire perspective, adding tasks to that goal that interfere with the company's profitability (e.g., making drugs more affordable, creating jobs for welfare mothers, achieving energy independence) seems impractical and gratuitous.

The laissez-faire outlook goes all the way back to Adam Smith in the eighteenth century. The assumption implicit in Adam Smith's doctrine of the "invisible hand" lies at the heart of the capitalist enterprise. The supermarket, the landlord, the electric utility provide you with food, shelter, and light, not out of the goodness of their hearts but in pursuit of their own self interest. In principle, business's single-minded pursuit of its self-interest and comparative advantage leads to maximum efficiency for each capitalist nation, augmenting the "wealth of [all] nations."

In recent years, the Economics Department at the University of Chicago has revitalized laissez-faire ideology. Why make an extra effort to reconcile profitability with good works when the pursuit of profitability, by its very nature, automatically produces good works? Loosen the bonds of regulation, leave business to its own devices, and as long as there is vigorous competition, the dynamism of the market will produce economic growth and by extension the societal well-being that people crave.

Laissez-faire doctrine assigns a major role to only two actors—enterprise owners and government. The role of government is to maintain a stable environment within which the enterprise can operate—a system of laws and regulations that ensure stability, property rights, prevention of monopoly, and provisions for "externalities" that go beyond the jurisdiction of any one company or industry (such as education, preservation of wilderness, clean air and water, and other aspects of the environment). Controversy swirls around where to draw the boundaries between business and government. Some advocates want government to do more, others want it to do less. But all share the assumption that the key accountable players are the owners and managers of business enterprises, with government representing the larger society.

If societies could count reliably on laissez-faire principles, there would be no need for stewardship ethics or the corporate social responsibility movement. The market would automatically produce the ethical results that society seeks to achieve. The West has now had several centuries of experience with free-market economies as well as with doctrines developed in opposition to them, like communism and socialism. What does that experience tell us? Overwhelmingly, it tells us that market economies are not fixed in character but vary from era to era and from culture to culture. Their inherent nature is far less clear-cut than either their advocates or opponents presuppose. We have learned that sometimes laissez-faire does work as Adam Smith and the Chicago School of Economics say it should, but that often it doesn't.

The brutal fact is that when we all pursue our own economic self-interest, the result is rarely the optimum social good. What Adam Smith discovered was a striking insight, not an iron law. Some of the time and under certain conditions it holds true. But it is exceedingly difficult to know in advance whether or not particular business decisions will add to—or subtract from—our overall well-being.

Consider just a few examples of recent business/economic decisions:

- In seeking to grow their profits, our nation's banks are offering a wide variety of mortgages that tempt people to buy homes they cannot afford. If the housing bubble bursts, we could easily repeat the savings and loan disaster of the 1980s, resulting in millions of people losing their homes and huge losses to the banks that may require government bailout.

- Over the four-year period from 1999 to 2003, Wall Street investment advisers received more than $126 million in fee income from United Airlines as the company followed the advisers' recommendation to shift its employee pension funds from safe and secure bonds timed to pay when the pensions came due to stocks. Their incentive: to reduce the company's contribution to the pension plan. The sad result was catastrophic for the pension plan and the employees who counted on it for their retirement. The advisers got richer.[1]

- The writer/columnist Tom Friedman describes Congress's 2005 energy bill: "We are about to pass an energy bill that . . . will make no real dent in our gasoline consumption, largely because no

> one wants to demand that Detroit build cars that
> get much better mileage. We are just feeding De-
> troit the rope to hang itself. It's assisted suicide. I
> thought people went to jail for that."[2]

Laissez-faire has proven an unreliable guide for aligning the interests of business with those of the larger society.

Corporate Social Responsibility

Most laissez-faire supporters endorse business ethics including honesty, decency, fairness, and giving good value for the
money. They associate these with sound management and see
no need to single them out for special attention or to give them
a label that might somehow differentiate them from everyday
good business practice.

The advocates of corporate social responsibility take a
different stance. They believe that ethical issues *should* be given
special attention, a distinctive name and label, and be clearly
and sharply differentiated from everyday business practice.
This is what the corporate social responsibility movement
(CSR) is designed to do. Rather than seeing owners and government as the only actors, as the laissez-fairists do, CSR advocates see important roles for other "stakeholders": employees, customers, suppliers, NGOs, other representatives of civil
society, and the entire developing world in its struggle to escape from poverty and misery.

The CSR movement has been around since the 1960s.
The emerging global economy has given it new vigor, and it is
currently exercising considerable influence, especially in Europe and Canada. Even in the United States it has taken on a
new dynamism.

The goal of CSR is to persuade corporations to adhere to a "triple bottom line," with equal weight given to:

- Corporate profitability
- Sustainable development (for example, protecting the environment)
- Societal well-being (for example, the rights of workers, social justice)[3]

This model is grounded in an implicit assumption that the fundamental premise of laissez-faire is wrong, and that the pursuit of profit (the traditional bottom line) is unlikely to advance the society's interest in sustainability or communal well-being. To correct this flaw, CSR layers new ethical obligations on top of this bottom line—additional responsibilities that seriously limit CSR's appeal to the corporate world.

The January 22, 2005, issue of *The Economist* provides us with insight into why the business sector has so much trouble in wholeheartedly embracing CSR. *The Economist* devoted a fourteen-page special section—"The Good Company"—to a discussion of corporate social responsibility.

The section starts by exclaiming how popular and successful CSR has become. "On the face of it," the article states, "this marks a significant victory in the battle of ideas." It is a victory, however, that *The Economist* deplores. Though *The Economist* editor who wrote the section, Clive Crook, finds some good in the CSR movement, his overall judgment is harsh. "Capitalism does not need the fundamental reform that many CSR advocates wish for it," he writes. And he accuses CSR's advocates of advancing "a mistaken analysis of how to serve the public good." He concludes bluntly, "The thinking behind CSR gives an account . . . which is muddled, and in some important ways, downright false."

CSR's many legitimate and responsible demands leave Crook in a quandary. He rejects the movement because he believes its basic premises are false, but at the same time he has to concede that much of what CSR is asking makes good business sense and sometimes can add value for investors. Fortunately, in the middle of the special section Crook proposes a simple and fair test for judging CSR—and stewardship ethics as well. He writes that putting arguments about motives, tone, intentions and everyday management duties aside, and "thinking only of results," he would like to pose two questions to all acts of "supposedly enlightened corporate citizenship":

1. Does it improve the company's long-term profitability?
2. Does it advance the broader public good?

I welcome these two questions. They constitute sound criteria for demands made on the business sector. Moreover, the answers to these two questions constitute a strong justification for stewardship ethics. The cardinal point about stewardship ethics is that it squarely meets both criteria while, as *The Economist* laments at great length, CSR meets only one.[4]

As I have shown in previous chapters, neither laissez-faire nor CSR seems to be successful at stopping the scandals. The unpleasant reality is that the explosion of business scandals happened under the aegis of these two frameworks. The laissez-faire framework—with its assumption that honesty, integrity, and value for the money are part of ordinary business practice—has proven impotent to halt or slow the scandals. And CSR hasn't done much better. Many of its corporate advocates (like Citigroup and Fannie Mae and Time Warner and the former smooth-talking Enron) have found themselves enmeshed in the scandals.

A strong argument for stewardship ethics is that the two current contenders in the battle of economic ideas failed to prevent the scandals, failed to explain their occurrence, and failed to offer a viable strategy for preventing them from happening in the future. These are large failures. Unless overcome, they will lead to deepening mistrust and to the recurring crises of confidence that have rocked capitalist economies in the past.

In what follows I identify the core features of stewardship ethics and outline the main elements that distinguish it from the other two frameworks.

Stewardship Ethics as Caring

It is the practice of many hospitals to charge people without health insurance much higher rates for the same services than they charge those who have insurance. Since most people without insurance are poor, the result is that the well-to-do are charged lower fees and the poor higher fees for the same services. Because poor people are often unable to pay the exorbitant prices that hospitals charge, many hospitals have harnessed the power of government to enforce payment by garnisheeing wages and using other methods of law enforcement to get their money. It is no accident that fully half of all personal bankruptcies in recent years have been caused by the costs associated with illness.

So unmanageable have health care costs become for Americans who lack health insurance or whose health insurance does not cover the mounting costs of drugs that people have tried to import their drugs from Canada at reduced prices. But they have encountered a formidable obstacle: the chairman of the nation's largest drug company, Pfizer, has led the lobbying effort in Congress to prevent such importation. He has even argued that his reason is concern for people's safety (the Canadians, of course, being such notorious crooks, cheats, and con artists).

These examples highlight the opposite of stewardship ethics; they exemplify *anti*stewardship ethics. They help us to pinpoint the core element of stewardship ethics, which is *caring*. A company's stewardship ethics dictates *whom* it cares for and *how* that care is given. It prescribes various ways that business leaders can take care of the institutions and people in their orbit of concern. Whatever it is that hospitals who hound the poor into bankruptcy care about, the economic plight of poor patients is not part of their caring. Whoever it is that Pfizer may care about, it's not the average hard-pressed American.

This does not mean that the hospitals and Pfizer are irresponsible villains out to exploit whomever they can for their own profit. Most hospitals are in a terrible bind. Because our country has not solved the problem of what to do about the 44 million Americans who lack health insurance, the hospitals have become the default solution. Poor people who are sick go to hospital emergency rooms because they have no other place to go. Our society cannot expect our overburdened hospital system to pick up the tab for a society-wide problem.

Notwithstanding the hospitals' excuse—and it is a good one—the fact remains that in relation to poor people who cannot pay their bills, these institutions bring to bear the opposite of stewardship ethics. Why should hospitals charge poor people more—a great deal more—for their services than they charge well-off people? This unintended consequence may fit into a bureaucratic arrangement where those with insurance have gotten price breaks for themselves, and the hospitals are making up for the loss by boosting prices for lower-income people who don't have that leverage. This is what I mean by antistewardship ethics—a lack of caring that permits abuses to go unheeded, or even causes the abuses.

The case of Pfizer is a little different. From a laissez-faire point of view, Pfizer may be pursuing sound business practice in safeguarding the extra profits it makes by charging Americans much more than Canadians for the same drugs. Except that Pfizer could hardly find a more shortsighted policy to pursue if it tried. The profits that Pfizer will forfeit in the future due to its damaged reputation will far exceed the profits it is now booking from its present double-standard pricing policy. Indeed, the current low level of Pfizer's stock price is already reflecting fallout from its leadership of the anti-import lobbying effort. There are high costs associated with violating the unwritten rules of stewardship ethics.

Pfizer gives the impression that it simply does not care about the plight of those victimized by its short-term profit-maximizing policies. It acts as if it was blindsided by the public's negative reaction. It sponsored a series of television ads featuring its chairman emphasizing what a caring company Pfizer is. This situation sums up everything that is wrong with how some companies are dealing with ethics: they are using expensive forms of public relations to spin the crassest of self-serving actions and to pass themselves off as ethically responsible companies.

In their own eyes, such companies unquestionably see themselves in this favorable light. This is because they are so highly selective in choosing the objects of their care. They care deeply about some constituencies (shareholders, doctors, the

FDA) while remaining indifferent to others (the uninsured and everyone needing to keep health care costs under control).

Stewardship ethics is also selective in choosing whom to care for and how to apply that care. It has to be. Indiscriminate caring is a formula for disaster and the loss of profitability. The key to selectivity lies in the company's understanding of its own enlightened self-interest. The former Procter and Gamble CEO John Pepper writes about his early years at P&G when one experience after another conveyed to him the depth of the company's commitment to the consumer and its needs and values.[5] Starbucks realized early on that its enlightened self-interest lay in treating its employees well so that they, in turn, would be friendly and hospitable to customers. Companies like Loral Space and Communications, a satellite manufacturer, and IBM, a pioneering manufacturer of mainframe computers, realized that their enlightened self-interest lay in providing top-level service to customers *after* the customer purchased the product. These big-ticket, temperamental, prone-to-breakdown products require the utmost in aftercare to keep the anxieties of their customers at bay.

These days, companies do not often stop to ask themselves where their enlightened self-interest really should lead them. They simply assume that they know the answer, or they take their cues from the numbers—return on investment, growth rate, year-over-year profit increases. But these quantitative cues are only a rearview mirror: they are not enough to help a company face the future. Detroit has always prided itself on giving buyers the kinds of cars they want at that particular moment, but it rarely pauses to look ahead to the future. U.S. automobile manufacturers were unprepared for the small-car challenge from Japan in the 1970s in the aftermath of the Arab oil embargo, just as they are currently unprepared for the energy crunch of the coming decades. They care about their immediate profitability even if it leads to long-term loss of market share; they seem oblivious to where their own enlightened self-interest lies.

The task of choosing the right form of caring involves judgment and a high level of leadership skill. The American Red Cross got into serious trouble by making the wrong call about the resources that poured into its headquarters in the aftermath of the 9/11 attacks. Red Cross executives decided to set aside a portion of the public's contributions for the organization's own institutional needs and for use against future disasters. Contributors who had intended to aid the 9/11 victims were furious. Top-level Red Cross officials were forced to resign. Critics accused the Red Cross of putting its own bureaucratic needs ahead of its mission.

A more sympathetic interpretation would be that Red Cross officials were torn between two conflicting forms of caring for their institution: caring for its immediate mission in relation to 9/11 and caring for its ability to carry out its mission in the future. Under less emotional circumstances, its decision might have been regarded as an act of prudence rather than bureaucratic obtuseness and insensitivity.

This type of conflict is central to stewardship. Does the good steward look out first and foremost for its stakeholders or for institutional needs of the organization? The argument in favor of the institutional priority is simple: for an organization to perform its function, it has to exist, and if it doesn't attend to its institutional needs, it may cease to exist. This is not an argument that one should carelessly brush aside. But neither does it justify most bureaucratic decisions. The world is full of organizations and institutions that continue to exist without performing their functions well: no one is well served when the drive for institutional survival overwhelms the basic mission of the organization.

Sometimes caring takes the form of choosing between alternatives that may have roughly equal merits on economic grounds, but not on political or social grounds. The economic thinker Norton Garfinkle describes an important example. In the United States at the present time, two economic theories—supply-side economics and demand-side economics—compete for dominance in shaping our nation's tax policies. The logic of the supply-siders holds that the best way to stimulate economic growth is through the capital formation that comes from lowering the tax burden on the nation's wealthiest people. The logic of the demand-siders is that the best way to stimulate economic growth is to leave as much money as possible in the hands of the broad mass of people, who in spending it stimulate job creation and investments in new plant and equipment.

From a strictly economic point of view, both hypotheses are equally plausible and subject to empirical testing. From the point of view of civil society, however, they are far from equal. The trickle-down dynamic of supply-side tax policy leads to an ever-widening income gap between the haves and the have-nots, violating tenets of fairness as the rich get richer and the middle class gets hollowed out.

Garfinkle has tested the two theories. His tests challenge the claims of supply-siders that their approach to capital formation leads to more vigorous economic growth. Indeed, his empirical research supports the conclusion that demand-side approaches may be more effective than supply-side ones from an economic as well as a societal standpoint. Garfinkle concludes:

> If, under the influence of supply-side economic policies, income inequality continues to grow, and

America evolves from a middle-class society into an asymmetrical "hourglass economy"—with a few at the top, many at the bottom, and ever-fewer in the middle—it will be increasingly difficult to sustain the belief that Americans share a common destiny that outweighs the differences that divide them. The belief in fairness will wither, and with it the sense of democratic community. In the end, such a future will spell the demise of the American dream.

Supply-side policies that contribute to increasing inequality between the richest Americans and middle-class Americans are therefore not only counterproductive to economic growth; they are counterproductive to sustaining the middle-class foundation of our American democracy. Demand-side economic policies not only contribute to economic growth—they also contribute to the continuing strength and stability of our American democracy and the survival of the American dream.[6]

In this example, Garfinkle faults supply-side theories for their economic as well as their societal flaws. But even if supply-side theory were equal or even marginally superior to the demand-side approach in purely economic terms, it fails badly on the criterion of serving our political and social needs. In our terms of reference, therefore, it violates stewardship ethics.

Community

A key aspect of caring relates to the reality that today's giant corporations are communities as well as enterprises designed to carry out a specific business function. How well a company conceives and executes stewardship ethics as a community has a direct bearing on its long-term profitability. A supermarket chain, Wegmans, comes to mind as exemplary.

Wegmans, an eighty-nine-year-old grocery chain, was named first on *Fortune* magazine's 2005 list of best companies to work for. *Fortune* describes the company as "that rare breed: a grocer beloved by its employees."

Wegmans goes out of its way to listen to its employees and heed their suggestions, making the people who work there, however lowly their jobs, feel that they are part of management. The ethos of the organization is to respect and empower employees. Wegmans's workers are encouraged to do whatever is necessary, on the spot, without consulting a higher-up. It is "an environment where workers can shine, unburdened by hierarchies." So a bakery employee can introduce a new cookie that she has been making for other employees. Reports are not channeled through levels of supervisors but given directly to top management. Jack DePeters, the operations chief, observes dryly: "We are a $3 billion company run by 16-year-old cashiers."[7]

In an industry notorious for labor/management strife, strikes, mistrust, and menial jobs, this grocery chain has, through working assiduously to create a sense of community with its employees, created a form of stewardship ethics that is good for profits as well as for customers, employees, and the community. Wegmans pays well, pursues family friendly policies, and walks the walk as well as talking the talk.

Higher Expectations

There is another dimension of caring associated with stewardship ethics. It is the recognition that with greater privilege goes greater responsibility. The French call it noblesse oblige, and we in the United States think of it as "meeting higher expectations." The principle here is that those with greater access to resources, power, and influence have a special stewardship obligation to serve the wider society.

In my Introduction, I quoted Wal-Mart's CEO, who stated that he had been shocked by Wal-Mart's critics into acknowledging the legitimacy of this principle. Many of our elite institutions and successful individuals embody this principle—Harvard University, the Ford Foundation, Bill Gates, Trinity Church of New York, and so on. It is violations of the unwritten rules of higher expectations that make companies like Pfizer look so bad. Because it is the largest and richest of the drug companies, more is expected of its leadership—a broader orbit of concern than one might expect from smaller, less powerful, less well-heeled companies. Pfizer should be leading the way to discover new policies and methods for making drugs more affordable for everyone rather than leading the way to making them less affordable. Stewardship ethics is as simple and straightforward as that.

Recognition of higher expectations stretches goals for organizations. It expands their orbit of caring. The main focus of the 2005 meeting of top executives at Davos, Switzerland, concerned the broadest possible orbit for business—the opportunities and responsibilities of the rich nations of the world to bring the five billion or so poor people in the developing world into the market economy—to make profitable consumers out of the billions of people now subsisting on one or two dollars a day or less.

Davos participants had the creative imagination to explore how a combination of technology, entrepreneurship, sheer market power, and goodwill might enable nations to become profitable markets and viable societies. The methods of realizing this sort of bold vision are varied. One of the most promising is the microlending that the Grameen Bank of Bangladesh pioneered. Now mainstream banks like Citigroup have expanded their microlending efforts in Mexico and India and have come to see them as potentially profitable long-term business opportunities. Procter and Gamble is experimenting with low-cost water purification methods in developing nations. Hewlett-Packard is seeking new ways of bringing technology to third-world countries, opening up new markets.

In sum, the caring aspect of stewardship takes multiple forms—caring about performance, caring about employees and customers, caring about the business as a community, and taking on special responsibilities because you have the means and resources to do so. But stewardship ethics also sets priorities among these various forms of caring—priorities that put performance ahead of bureaucratic needs and that seek to leave the company under its care better off.

Stewardship Ethics and CSR

At a casual glance, this formulation of stewardship ethics may seem a great deal like corporate social responsibility (CSR).

On the surface, stewardship ethics is certainly closer to CSR than it is to laissez-faire. Like stewardship ethics, CSR also involves caring and expanding its orbit to include those who have been excluded. And in recent years, CSR has been moving in the direction of stewardship ethics. However, stewardship ethics does differ from CSR in several crucial ways—most fundamentally in its attitude toward profits. It is this difference that makes stewardship ethics more likely to be accepted and implemented by the business sector.

When CSR first appeared in the United States several decades ago, most of its advocates came from outside the business sector. They pressed insistent demands on corporations that were often unrealistic and subversive of the corporation's business purpose of making a profit on the products and services it produced. Business leaders became so annoyed at the tone of moral self-righteousness of CSR's advocates that they often rejected CSR's legitimate and responsible demands as well as its unreasonable ones.

CSR and stewardship ethics arise from somewhat different value orientations. CSR advocates still come mainly from outside the business sector. Profit making does not enjoy a privileged position in their hierarchy of values: rather, it occupies a lowly spot, somewhere between discomfort and mild support. Whether a company makes a bigger or smaller profit— or any profit at all—is often not important to advocates of CSR. What matters most to them is promoting social good. The stewardship ethics position, on the other hand, shares the perspective of the business sector about profit making. It does not regard profit making as problematic. On the contrary, it appreciates the many uses to which profits may be put— including but not confined to—rewarding shareholders.

In their online paper "The Death of Environmentalism," two second-generation environmentalists give a blistering account of how the traditional environmentalist approach has weakened the movement. They take their colleagues to task for framing their demands on business in a manner that makes both jobs and profits secondary concerns, thereby mobilizing the resistance of unions as well as business management.[8] The point of their paper is that it is possible to align environmentalism with job creation and corporate profitability, though doing so will oblige advocates to challenge old assumptions and convictions. In effect, they are imploring the environmental movement to shift from a CSR orientation that is indifferent to jobs and profitability to a stewardship ethics code that searches for ways to meet strict economic criteria and care about civil society values at the same time.

A summary of the differences between the two perspectives is laid out in Figure 3.

The CSR movement is more active and effective than it was in the past—so much so that many major corporations feel obliged to give it at least token acknowledgement. But it has not changed the way most companies do business. For all its flaws, CSR's critique of current business practice serves a useful purpose. It places fundamental questions about the inherent nature of market economies squarely on the public agenda—in particular, the question of just how flexible markets are and how adaptable they can be to the ethical imperatives of the cultures in which they are embedded. As market capitalism spreads across the globe, one can hardly think of a timelier question.

Some parts of the business sector will take issue with the point of view I am urging here. But most will endorse it. Business managers learned early in their careers that a business must make a profit to succeed, but they also learned to think, feel, and act as citizens. They are pragmatists, not laissez-faire ideologues. Their self-respect is tied to their conviction that the roles of business executive and responsible citizen reinforce rather than contradict each other. They are proud to be businesspeople because they believe it makes them better Americans. And they believe their role as citizens enhances their suc-

CSR	Stewardship Ethics
Arises mainly from NGOs	Arises from within business
Social good has higher priority than profits	Profits are a necessary precondition
Attitudes toward profits are ambivalent	Profits regarded as both essential and ethically sound
Adds ethical burden to business goals	Reconciles caring and profitability
Assumes all good deeds are equally desirable	Assumes good deeds must also advance the company's core mission
An "add-on"—easy to meet as a charitable gesture	Requires genuine transformation

Figure 3. CSR vs. stewardship ethics

cess as businesspeople. They agonize over the difficult question of how to reconcile the conflicting pressures of contributing to society with short-term business pressures. The main question they will raise is not whether stewardship ethics is justified (the question *The Economist* raises about CSR) but whether such a high standard of ethics can be realized in today's harsh business environment; that is, whether stewardship ethics is practical from a strictly pragmatic point of view.

While most business leaders endorse the maxim that you can do well by doing good, not all of them truly believe it deep down. And even when they do, they are not sure how to carry it out it in practice under the day-to-day pressures of Wall Street. They surely have a point. A Pollyanna posture would be naïve in the extreme. Doing well by doing good is not a formula for a smooth and easy life. But for those willing to do the hard work, a stewardship ethics strategy opens a path that does reconcile long-term profitability with the greater public good.

VII

The Vision of Stewardship Ethics

What is a vision? The word has so many shades of meaning that I should specify how I am using it here. *Vision,* as I see it, is a way of articulating goals that seeks to overcome deeply ingrained negative practices. A vision in this sense is a word picture of what life would be like if we were able to stop or reverse an undesirable condition.

Martin Luther King Jr.'s "I Have a Dream" speech illustrates this meaning. King paints a picture of what life in the United States would be like if we were able to rid ourselves of racial prejudice and learn to live together in harmony. The European Union owes its existence to the vision of a united Europe free of the plague of wars, as enunciated by farsighted European statesmen in the aftermath of World War II. The software entrepreneur and philanthropist Bill Gates has a vision of what life would be like in the developing world if malaria and other curable diseases were eradicated.

To develop a stewardship ethics vision, I take as my point

of departure the debate of the past few decades between the vision of the free market and the vision of civil society, as described in Chapter 5. The two-visions debate has focused our attention on the tensions between the competitive demands of a global economy and the civil society values of fairness, community and concern for others—for a rising tide of economic well-being that raises all boats, not just the yachts. How to link our market economy to the values of civil society remains an achingly unresolved issue. Indeed, it is polarizing our political life.

The stewardship ethics vision in this book builds on the vision of the free market rather than starting with the vision of civil society. The reasons for this strategic choice are compelling. The vision of the free market has more traction with the American public than does the vision of civil society. Americans place an extraordinarily high value on material well-being as a precondition for personal freedom and self-fulfillment. In addition, with the advent of a truly global economy and the explosion of new technology, our market economy is probably the most dynamic sector of our society. And from a practical point of view, the probabilities of achieving meaningful reform in the business sector are far higher than in the sprawling and amorphous civil society sector. The business sector draws on vast resources of leadership, organization, and wealth: if there is a will to reform within the business sector, the resources to do so are available.

What follows, then, is a word picture of (1) how, ideally, our business sector would evolve under a robust vision of stewardship ethics and (2) what life in our society would be like if we were able to rescue current business practice from the forces creating the business scandals.

A Vision for the Business Sector

The year is 2007. The stewardship ethics movement starts slowly and quietly in two categories of companies. The larger category consists of companies that Wall Street calls "fallen angels"— companies whose once sky-high stock prices have plummeted and whose reputations have become tarnished. Scandal has wounded some of the fallen angels, like Shell, Fannie Mae, AIG, Merck, and Marsh and McLellan. Other fallen angels, like Altria and Monsanto, have suffered for other reasons—Altria because of its link with cigarettes, Monsanto because of its link with genetically modified organisms (which their opponents have termed "Frankenfoods").

In the boardrooms and management retreats of these companies, the conversation focuses incessantly on plans for rejuvenation. The most thoughtful executives realize that neither business-as-usual nor public relations spin will restore these companies to their past glory. If they are to regain their former standing, they will have to break old patterns. The executives begin to develop strategies for doing so.

The second category of reformers and innovators comprises leadership companies like G.E., Vanguard, Toyota, Dell, and Procter and Gamble, which see opportunities to broaden their lead over competitors even farther. They realize that reinforcing such ethical values as integrity, openness, and innovation will enhance their reputations and the value of their brand franchises. They continue to think "outside the box."

Both categories of companies start to ask new questions and to think in fresh ways about a new societal role for large corporations, a problem-solving role that is usually assigned to government or civil society. They focus on some of the unsustainable trends that are plaguing our societies, such as failure to achieve energy independence, rising health care costs and potentially disastrous climate change. Instead of seeking to profit from the problems they create without doing anything to alleviate them, they ask whether and how they can cope with them and whether, if they take a sufficiently long-term point of view, they can do so profitably. Aware of the limitations of governmental programs, they explore the constraints on their own resources and how they might work cooperatively with governments and civil society.

These companies are banking on specific products and processes. Toyota is an early exemplar. The company took big risks and may reap big rewards from its hybrid Prius models: automobiles powered by a combination of electricity and gasoline. In contrast to the consumer-unfriendly approach of taxing the price of gasoline to encourage fuel efficiency (adding hugely to the consumer's cost), Toyota has adopted a far more consumer-friendly strategy: a market approach that combines technology and entrepreneurship to enhance fuel efficiency and assist energy independence.

Procter and Gamble has carved out a similar pioneering approach to a very different problem. The company has developed an ingenious way to purify water using low-cost packets of powder (under the brand name Pür). Pür proved its social value in Sri Lanka in the aftermath of the 2004 tsunami. But its initial commercial launch lost money because the product is complicated to use and too costly for the poorest nations. The *Wall Street Journal* reports that when Procter and Gamble's CEO, A. G. Lafley, was given a list of the forty countries with the highest rates of infant mortality that could benefit most from its water purification methods, he committed the company to a twenty-year plan under which Pür will be introduced in two of these countries every year, starting with Haiti and

Uganda, until it covers all forty. Procter and Gamble intends to make Pür a long-term commercial success as well as a humanitarian contribution.[1]

On yet another gridlock issue, Shell, one of the fallen angels, has launched an ambitious plan to develop renewable energies to help offset the negative effects of global climate change. It is applying research and development resources to wind power and photovoltaics, partnering with conservation organizations throughout the world, providing loans to small entrepreneurs in the energy sector in Africa, and in many other ways assuming the lead in global climate change initiatives. In accepting an award from the World Environment Center, Shell's spokesman stated, "My colleagues and I are totally committed to a business strategy that generates profits while contributing to the well-being of the planet and its people."[2]

Other fallen angels have similar opportunities to put stewardship ethics into practice. Merck has been a victim both of its own ethical cross-pressures and of the harvest of ill will that its industry has reaped. The pharmaceutical industry has gained the reputation of being unable to contain its greed in raising drug prices as high as the traffic will bear, regardless of the company's actual costs. Consumers feel trapped: they need the drugs whether or not they can afford them, and they feel that the drug companies are insensitive to their plight. The big pharma companies justify the high prices they charge by stressing the high costs of new drug research. But it has long been an open secret that much of their costs come from expensive marketing and advertising campaigns rather than from scientific research.

While Merck has a long ethical tradition and outstanding devotion to quality and public service, it has faltered in this troubled environment. It was badly wounded by a series of actions in relation to its Vioxx pain reliever. It voluntarily withdrew Vioxx from the market in 2004 after learning that trials had shown that high doses of Vioxx over extended periods of time significantly increased the threat of heart attack. Critics claim that Merck has known about this problem with Vioxx for years but had failed to act because Vioxx was one of the company's most profitable products. Merck is embroiled in a series of lawsuits charging that Vioxx, even in small doses, brings on heart attacks.

Without the ill will toward its industry and the general mistrust of business stirred up by the accounting scandals, Merck might have been given the benefit of the doubt. But instead, in the aftermath of the Vioxx withdrawal, the company was sucked into the vortex of mistrust. Its stock plunged in value, its reputation for integrity was smeared, and its future profitability is threatened by multiple lawsuits.

Let us imagine a situation in which Merck realizes that the only way it can recoup its former standing and reputation is to take some dramatic initiative. After several years of policy research and analysis, it decides to offer new ideas for reforming the patent system for drugs on the grounds that the current system inflates the price of drugs for consumers. Present patent arrangements give drug companies a monopoly for a specified number of years on the sale of drugs they have developed and tested. Developing new drugs, testing them for years and agonizing over the approval process is quite costly, especially with a faltering success rate for new drugs. In recent years, most pharmaceutical companies have found themselves without a comforting supply of new drugs in the pipeline. Quite naturally, the companies feel pressured to squeeze whatever profits they can from their few successes before their patents expire and their drugs go generic. But in our scenario Merck decides to take leadership in proposing ideas for changes in the patent and review systems in the interest of lowering drug prices for consumers.

In 2008 Merck begins to propose key changes in the patent-and-review structure of the industry. Merck takes the position that if the interests of consumers are to be safe-guarded, the industry needs to reform the drug patent process so that companies are not forced to push prices ever higher during the limited period of patent protection. There is a vari-ety of ways to reform the process; for example, the period of patent protection might be linked to the magnitude of the com-pany's investment in developing the drug—admittedly, the metrics would be complex, but not impossibly so. Merck ar-gues that the industry's lack of concern with the impact of its actions on consumers generates a climate of mistrust and ill will that threatens the industry's own long-term profitability. It proposes changes that work in favor of consumers as well as the industry.

As the fallen angels and the leadership companies decide to invest in addressing difficult policy issues, their example in-spires others to take similar initiatives. Developing compelling and successful models that inspire other companies is perhaps the single best way to change norms for the better. The new model begins to catch on. Companies come to realize that it is sometimes necessary to focus their long-term profitability goals on projects that make enhancing the public good an explicit objective, rather than taking it for granted as an automatic byproduct of their search for profits.

In this vision, converging forces now work to advance ethical standards rather than weaken them. The wave of scan-dals serves as a learning experience and a wakeup call. Prolif-erating success stories demonstrate that stewardship ethics can be quite profitable. Executives realize that it means a lot to their employees and to their own self-respect and self-esteem. They learn how much competitive advantage they can gain through building and strengthening their companies' reputation for integrity and effective problem solving.

Perhaps the majority of companies will hold back initially out of fear of a negative stock market reaction. They will hesitate to move toward a better balance between short- and long-term profitability until the stock market starts to reward them for doing so. Eventually the market will reward them, because there are plenty of investors willing to invest in companies that practice stewardship ethics once they see that it makes good business sense to do so.

Several incentives will inspire companies to experiment with stewardship ethics and then, after seeing positive results, to embrace the new ethic enthusiastically. One is the negative motivation of avoiding the taint of scandal. Scandal is bad for business and bad for a company's pride and self-respect. The major incentive, though, is a positive one: through stewardship ethics corporations can gain two huge competitive benefits— significant improvement in employee commitment and stronger customer loyalty and goodwill—both assets of tremendous importance.

Employee Commitment

In my vision of stewardship ethics, employees are among the first to regain their trust in and loyalty to their employers. Companies discover that as stewardship ethics takes hold, employee commitment rises dramatically. As competition in the global economy grows more vigorous, corporations realize that a high level of employee commitment is indispensable to com-

petitive success. As this realization sinks in, companies give re-
newed attention to employee motivation and commitment—a
consideration that had been long neglected in most companies.

During the industrial era of assembly lines and strong
unions, companies paid scant attention to employee motivation. Most jobs did not require high levels of employee initiative and dedication. These were prerequisites of management.
But as our economy evolved, the nature of jobs changed slowly
but decisively. People were no longer hired, as one worker put
it, "from the neck down." Jobs demanded ever-higher levels of
"discretionary effort."[3]

The long-term trend in the United States shows a steady
increase in the number of high-discretion jobs—jobs that depend on the initiative of the jobholder. Before World War II,
only 18 percent of jobs could be characterized as high-discretion jobs—jobs requiring an extra measure of initiative that
depends on jobholder commitment. By 1982 that number had
increased to 43 percent, and by the new century it had risen to
62 percent.[4] In other words, as we outsource routine jobs, many
of the jobs that remain call for high levels of commitment. Our
competitive success in the global economy does not depend
solely on capital and technology; it depends critically on employee morale and commitment.

Unfortunately, the motivation systems of management
have lagged behind the need for higher levels of commitment.
My own research and that of the Gallup organization show that
employee commitment has long been stagnant. In the 1980s
fewer than one out of four of the nation's employees (22 percent) said they were willing to "give the best they had" to the
job (where they spend such a huge chunk of their life, time,
and energy). By the turn of the century, this low number had
further declined to 20 percent. An even more depressing find-

ing is the fact that the longer an employee stays with a company, the lower his or her level of commitment. After ten years, an employee's willingness to give the company the best he has had sunk even further. This widening gap is demonstrated in Figure 4.[5]

In the vision of stewardship ethics that I hope will come to pass, companies realize the high cost of low employee commitment, and they begin to address its major causes. The most important cause is employee perception that loyalty is a one-way street. Corporations expect their employees to be loyal to them but accept little reciprocal obligation toward their employees. Job security is a thing of the past. Employers realize that the conditions of the world economy do not permit them to guarantee job security. But they can surely do far more to help prepare their employees for frequent job change, through better career-path planning.

Even when it was still under the constraints of bankruptcy and had to let some employees go, Loral Space and Communications went to exceptional lengths to treat its departing employees well. As a result, when the company emerged from bankruptcy, many of those former employees eagerly returned. Loral's CEO, Bernard Schwartz, states plainly: "In a company like ours, care for employees must come first."

John Pepper, Procter and Gamble's former CEO, gives an excellent example of how in the new global economy a company can balance the efficiency needs of the business with the needs of employees for continuity of income and stability. Pepper writes that when Procter and Gamble started manufacturing operations near Tula in Russia, the productivity of the plant fell below that of other Procter and Gamble plants and had four times as many employees as it needed. The company knew that unemployment was high in the region and that laid-

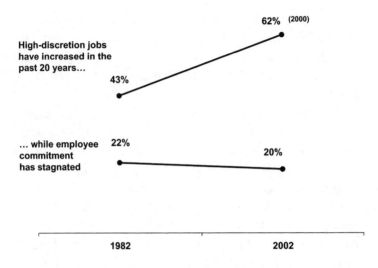

Figure 4. High-discretion jobs vs. employee commitment
1982–2002. Data from Yankelovich Partners and Gallup
tracking polls, 1982–2002.

off workers would have difficulty finding new employment.
Determined to manage the reduction in employment with respect and concern for its employees, Procter and Gamble
helped to set up a number of small, stand-alone enterprises for
some of its products such as aerosols and linoleum flooring,
plus a training center (the first of its kind in the region), plus
generous retirement packages for those who wished to retire.
In this way the company responded both to the business imperative to downsize when necessary and to the community
imperative to care for its employees to the best of its capabilities and resources.[6]

  In the vision proposed here, instead of job loss automatically being a trauma, employers learn how to help jobholders
experience it as a challenge and opportunity for self-better-

ment. They assist employees in overcoming the experience of loss, helplessness, long periods of unemployment, and pressure to accept lower levels of pay and work. Training, education, and career planning for new jobs as well as existing ones become a more important corporate activity. The new post of chief education officer enjoys high standing and importance.

Companies also acknowledge the strong motivating power of giving employees a voice in the decisions that affect their jobs and are responsive to their suggestions. Executives grow less possessive about their managerial prerogatives and less rigid about status differences. They begin to understand that the rules of creating community are different from the rules of managing a hierarchical company, and they learn how to integrate the two. They realize that doing so is a matter primarily not of technical skills but of attitude and of coping with status anxiety. They learn that as soon as they stop worrying about their own status and start treating their employees as equals, their status becomes more secure, not less.

Companies also pay more attention to family-friendly policies of flextime and work at home. They begin especially to shape new policies for the health care of their employees. When employees are overwhelmed by family illness (especially if children are involved), the company should use all of its resources to help the family. An important part of employee loyalty and commitment grows out of companies' new approaches to health care. Instead of the steady erosion of employee goodwill caused by annual increases in copayments and other restrictions, companies create a new climate of partnership between management and employees in managing health care costs and working cooperatively with unions in companies that have them. Given a voice in shaping health care strategies, and time to study and adapt models of how other companies have succeeded in overcoming the monster of ever-rising health care costs, employees gradually abandon their traditional entitlement psychology in favor of sharing responsibility for controlling the costs of their health care even when the company is paying for a large part of it.

Consumer Goodwill

The vision of stewardship ethics also encompasses the prospect of building stronger relationships with customers. Enhancing customer loyalty to the brand is probably the single most powerful incentive for convincing companies to adopt stewardship ethics as a way of life. Building consumer loyalty, though extremely valuable, is difficult to accomplish. It usually cannot be done through good deeds unrelated to the company's products and services. Reading about G.E.'s efforts to alleviate poverty in Ghana, a typical consumer's reaction may be, "that's nice," but that same consumer will then go out and buy a competitor's light bulbs because they are ten cents cheaper. As companies know well, good deeds unrelated to the brand are for all practical purposes secondary or tertiary factors in the consumer's calculus of pros and cons for choosing among competitive brands. A half-century of market research testifies to the truth of this bit of worldly reality.

But good deeds directly related to the benefits the product delivers are another matter. These count—and count a lot. Decades after it occurred, Johnson and Johnson's swift and costly action to ensure the safety of its Tylenol analgesic after its packaging had been tampered with continues to pay dividends in terms of consumer loyalty and goodwill. Starbucks' commitment to set goals for sustainable agriculture developed better relations with coffee farmers and appealed to consumers' sense of fair play and environmental responsibility, bolstering the company's reputation.

Making a company's public policy initiatives a positive influence in consumer brand choice, as in the hypothetical Merck example, is a new development. It has not been important in the past because consumers rarely had occasion to applaud corporate intervention in public affairs. Consumers had grown accustomed to industry lobbyists working against their interests, not for them. Detroit routinely opposes consumer demands for greater fuel efficiency. The insurance industry is accustomed to lobbying hard for regulations that permit them to raise rates, whether or not these are justified by higher costs. In the 1980s and 1990s, banks, accounting firms, and brokerage companies fought successfully for the deregulation that loosened the safeguards preventing fraud. These loose standards heightened the temptations on executives that inevitably led to the rash of accounting scandals.

With the widespread adoption of stewardship ethics, corporate policy begins to shift in favor of consumer interests. Some companies now lobby for policies that benefit their customers as well as themselves. And as this new reality seeps into public consciousness, pro-consumer companies begin to win greater consumer loyalty, especially when consumers see a direct benefit to themselves flowing from the company's policies.

With their more active participation on public policy, companies also develop a new relationship to government. If many fewer companies are implicated in accounting scandals, the public will be more willing to accept the "few bad apples" thesis. On the positive side, the public will begin to recognize and to honor individual companies for their contributions to solving our most obdurate problems. Stewardship awards for business might take their place alongside of Oscar and the

Tony awards and honors for exceptional military service. The awards can be designed so that companies receiving them gain a distinct competitive edge.

In this vision, the public approves the evolving relationship between business and government. The relationship is not that of partners: the two types of organizations are too disparate to permit genuine partnership. Rather, what evolves is an increasingly clear division of effort. The public expresses its strong preference for market forces to take charge of some aspects of public life, such as delivering health care services and building large infrastructure projects, and for the government to take charge of other aspects, such as assuming responsibility for standards and safety nets.

Gradually, the old antagonism between business and government is replaced by arm's-length mutual respect. Political alignments are transformed, with liberals in Congress supporting companies that have extended themselves to serve public well-being and conservatives denouncing corporate intervention in public policy.

Slowly but inexorably, public attitudes toward the business sector begin to change for the better. The climate of mistrust dissipates, replaced by increasing respect and trust. This has happened several times in the past, but this time the trust and respect reach unprecedented levels. America's leading corporations become the most trusted and respected institutions in the nation. This is the vision of stewardship ethics.

VIII
What to Do about
Shareholder Value

To make room for stewardship ethics it will be necessary to address and reform the two business norms that are directly linked to the scandals—shareholder value and deregulation of laws that discourage conflicts of interest. This chapter focuses on shareholder value.

A Semantic Misunderstanding

The doctrine of shareholder value has become highly controversial and polarizing. Its advocates support it passionately; its opponents denounce it with equal fervor. Its advocates assume that those who oppose it must be naïve antibusiness liberals; its opponents assume that its supporters must be greedy, blind, or indifferent to its abuses.

Ironically, much of the controversy arises from mere semantic confusion. It turns out that advocates and opponents focus on different aspects of shareholder value, so that each side uses the same term to refer to something quite different. Advocates define shareholder value by its intent, which is to align the interests of the managers of corporations more closely with those of the corporation's "owners": its shareholders. This is a desirable objective—when the interests of both parties are focused on the long-term health of the company. The proponents of shareholder value take this long-term focus for granted; they assume that for its own future well-being, a company will want to be responsive to its employees, customers, and the public, and that this is the best way to realize true shareholder value.

When its opponents look at shareholder value, however, they see a radically different phenomenon. They see shareholder value as it actually works in practice, and they see that its customary practice makes a mockery of the original intent. Managers, these opponents say, have debased and hijacked the concept of shareholder value to enrich themselves. They do so by linking their compensation to the share price of the company's stock, which they then manipulate by managing earnings and playing other accounting tricks.

Opponents also see Wall Street as complicit in some of the worst abuses of shareholder value, as mutual funds, brokerage firms, and hedge funds position themselves as the "owners" of the stock and maintain that their interests should take precedence over those of employees, customers, and the public. Though these big funds and brokerage firms may momentarily hold shares, they do not act like owners who care about the company, and they do not hesitate to dump the stock at the slightest provocation. In theory, shareholder value is supposed to advance the long-term interests of the company. In practice, it often does the opposite. It is the long-term interests of the company that get sacrificed in its name.

If pressed, supporters of shareholder value might agree that the debased version of the principle has gained traction in recent years, but they do not want to lose sight of its original goals. The opponents of shareholder value have no quarrel with these goals but feel that the perversions of shareholder value are so deeply entrenched that they undermine whatever positive benefit the concept might once have had.

It is with this semantic clarification in mind that I argue that getting rid of the debased version of shareholder value is a useful first step in moving toward stewardship ethics. This debased version of shareholder value is one of the major driving forces behind the scandals that have bedeviled the business sector, besmirched its reputation, and undermined its ethical standards.

Just listen to the artful rhetoric of one of the most notorious hijackers of shareholder value, "Chainsaw Al" Dunlap. In discussing who the beneficiaries of shareholder value should be, Dunlap, a corporate raider of the 1990s, insists that its real intent is to benefit the small shareholder. "I'm not talking about Wall Street fat cats," he says. "Working people and retired men and women have entrusted us with their 401Ks and pension plans for their children's college tuition and their own long-term security. If we're not concerned about them every step of the way, they're screwed."[1]

And screwed they have been. In practice, shareholder value has hurt millions of small shareholders. Just ask the shareholders of Sunbeam and Scott Paper, which Chainsaw Al personally drove into bankruptcy. Or the shareholders of Enron or WorldCom or Tyco or Adelphia or the many other companies that claimed to be acting in the name of shareholder value while their executives enriched themselves at the expense of the smaller shareholders and endangered the survival of their organizations.

From LBOs to Stock Options

Leveraged buyouts (LBOs) were the first method of perverting the purpose of shareholder value. Through the use of credit (and the collusion of bankers), raiders like Dunlap acquired enough stock in companies like Scott Paper and Sunbeam to take control of them, load the companies with debt, fire a lot of people, cut expenses to the bone, enrich the new owners, and leave the denuded company to its fate—bankruptcy, or at the very least, severe loss of market momentum and position.

In the dotcom boom of the nineties, executive stock options replaced LBOs as the dominant expression of shareholder value—the mechanism for tying managerial rewards directly to the price of the company's stock. This was the second, and far more damaging, method of perverting shareholder value. And it caught on quickly. In 1980 only 33 percent of executives received stock options as part of their incentive package. Within a short fifteen years, that number had risen to a 70 percent majority. By the end of the twentieth century, CEOs of the largest corporations were receiving mega–options packages with an average value of $31 million. The ratio between CEO compensation and worker salary grew from 40 to 1 to more than 600 to 1. Shareholder value heaps immense wealth on corporate managers whether or not their performance warrants it. As the *Wall Street Journal*'s Jesse Eisinger has noted: "Spiraling CEO pay has become dangerously de-linked from performance."[2]

The *New York Times* reports a study that suggests that mega–option grants invite executives to take big risks that often go bad. The bigger the option grant, the "more likely that companies will fudge their numbers and that companies with such grants are more likely to go broke."[3] Jack McAllister, former CEO of US West (the Baby Bell that provides telephone service to fourteen western states) writes, "Employee contracts that insured huge amounts to management if a change in ownership happened has also been a negative influence. Many managers have been motivated to find a way to sell their company—to the disadvantage of employees and customers."[4]

It is important to note that the present form of shareholder value is not a long-held principle of market capitalism. Two economists, Michael Jensen and William Meckling, developed the concept in its present form only about thirty years ago. They believed that it would enhance the long-term profitability of companies. Instead, to their later shock and surprise, it gave rise to the cult of seeking to exceed the short-term earnings expectations of Wall Street analysts. As the *New Yorker* writer John Cassidy observes,

> Stock options, instead of spurring corporate leaders to build businesses that would create wealth for decades to come, encouraged them to manage for the short term, tailoring their actions to the demands of Wall Street stock analysts; and, in all too many cases, the practice turned them into crooks. . . . Senior executives who converted to the new religion of shareholder value tended to get very rich, while those who argued that corporations ought to consider their employees and customers as well as their shareholders often ended up without a job.[5]

At the time, Jensen and Meckling believed that shareholder value would actually raise the level of ethics in business by discouraging executives from indulging in expensive perks and building monuments to themselves at the shareholder's expense. This proved an exceedingly naïve assumption. Their doctrine of shareholder value opened the floodgates to executive self-serving. Michael Jensen has become so personally disillusioned that he now refers to stock options as "managerial heroin."[6]

Why did this well-intentioned concept become so distorted and perverted in its day-to-day application? It happened, at least in part, because economic theories do not get implemented in a vacuum. Ideas for changing the economy or the society are always launched in a dense context—a specific historical/cultural/political setting. It is the context that shapes what happens to the idea. This is especially true of economic ideas. Our economic lives are never isolated from the concreteness of our daily existence. The tendency of economists to wall off economics from its cultural/political/psychological context is the weakest part of economic theory.

Shareholder value might have had a different fate had it taken hold just a generation earlier, in the era during which the Pru regarded life insurance as a "sacred trust" and the Harvard Business School's class of 1949 felt totally grounded in the ethical absolutes of their parents. My own personal experience in the business world of that era leads me to believe that the same theory of shareholder value, implemented a generation earlier, might have kept better faith with the economists' emphasis on the long-term interests of the company.

It is possible, for example, to design stock option incentives in such a way that the payoff for a CEO comes mainly after he retires. This kind of option plan would resonate with the stewardship credo of leaving the company in better shape than it was when the CEO's watch began. Most of the CEOs I knew in that era would have found these kinds of long-term options totally compatible with their values. But they are not compatible with the winning-for-myself, instant gratification norms of some contemporary CEOs.

The worst features of our popular culture have seeped into the corporation: Look out for Number One. . . . Win at any cost. . . . If we want it, we get it. . . . I'm judged by whether I make more than the other guy. . . . Now that I'm CEO, I get to call the shots. . . . I let my lawyers worry about conflicts of interest. . . . If it's not illegal I didn't do anything wrong. . . . It's fun to game the system. . . . Whatever happens I must not lose. . . .

This psychology is powerfully reinforced by pressure that companies meet Wall Street's expectations for quarterly earnings. And it is further reinforced by the size of the rewards. There is a widespread feeling in business that everyone has his price, and when the price comes in the form of tens of millions of dollars, it grows hard to resist. This is especially the case when a convenient rationale like shareholder value can convince its beneficiaries that they deserve every cent of the millions of dollars they gain.

If shareholder value has been so thoroughly debased, why does it continue to enjoy such widespread popularity and support? It would be folly to underestimate the staying power of this doctrine and the firm grip it holds on both the corporate community and the legal and economic professions that support it. The law professor and economist Margaret Blair applauds the effort to replace what she calls "shareholder primacy" with the broader and more fundamental goal of encouraging corporate officers and directors to pursue the long-term success of the company. But she doubts that it will

happen because shareholder value is so firmly entrenched.
She writes:

> The notion that corporations are creatures of con-
> tract whose sole function is maximizing value for
> shareholders is so entrenched in the business com-
> munity, in MBA programs, in the business press,
> and in legal practice, that advocates of a broader
> view have a very difficult time being heard and
> taken seriously. . . . It's going to take a massive shift
> in the norms that have driven academic scholars
> and legal practice for the past two decades.[7]

Currently, business thought leaders are too invested in the
shareholder-value paradigm to subject it to the unsparing critique it needs. Yet as the need for that critique becomes clearer,
my surmise is that those with a vested interest in the theory
will find a way to fudge the issue. Many will redefine, broaden,
and qualify the theory until its central point—that shareholders
should always get preferential treatment—becomes so fuzzy as
to lose its meaning. In that way, the principle's one-time defenders can finesse their position, in effect abandoning the
theory without losing face or admitting error.

This development would leave the major beneficiaries of
shareholder value—CEOs and other top-level executives—as
its primary defenders. Many executives embrace shareholder
value simply because it makes them rich. Why, then, should
they abandon this welcome jackpot for a policy like stewardship ethics that presumably will make them less rich? Unless
the answer to that tantalizing question is credible, it will be exceedingly difficult to replace shareholder value with stewardship ethics.

Is Stewardship Ethics an Acceptable Substitute for Shareholder Value?

Asking CEOs to shift from shareholder value to stewardship ethics need not, in fact, demand great personal sacrifice on their part. Stewardship does not require a vow of poverty. There is no reason why CEOs and other top executives cannot be well rewarded for stewardship success. But the shift will call upon them to link their wealth aspirations more firmly to the long-term health and strength of the corporation. Ironically, stewardship ethics has a better chance to achieve the goals that shareholder value originally set for itself and has miserably failed to achieve.

Under shareholder value the link between the CEO's financial incentives and the company's well-being has proven feeble at best. When CEO rewards are tied to short-term earnings, things often go badly awry. For example, based on reported 2001 earnings of $93 million, El Paso gave its CEO a $10 million bonus. A few years later in restating its earnings for 2001, the company reported that it had actually suffered a $447 million loss! But it failed to get its former CEO to return his huge bonus. This same pattern repeats itself whenever companies are forced to restate earnings. A March 13, 2005, *New York Times* story aptly headlined, "Sorry, I'm Keeping the Bonus Anyway," lists Dynegy, Nortel, Qwest, Xerox, Computer Associates, Bristol-Myers Squibb, Tyco, and Time Warner as examples of companies that gave their CEOs huge bonuses linked to earnings that were later proven illusory; few of these companies managed to get the money back.

Unlike Tyco's Dennis Kozlowski, most CEOs are not big spenders. They are not high-livers demanding yachts and mansions and cadres of servants. The careers they chose—as hard-

working, hard-driving executives—leave neither time nor opportunity nor inclination for sybaritic self-indulgence. Life at
the top is a calling, and callings demand total commitment.
Beyond a certain level, a CEO's wealth becomes a symbol, a way
of keeping score. CEOs are fiercely competitive. At present,
their main method for judging how well they are doing is to
measure how much money they are rewarded in comparison
to their peers.

The constant ratcheting up of CEO rewards started just
a few decades ago. The process now works something like this:

The Compensation Committee of the Board hires outside
consultants to take on the dicey issue of how to compensate
the CEO—the very person who selected the board's members
and who is likely to be a friend or associate. The consultants
prepare charts and graphs full of comparative data. Invariably,
the charts lead to the conclusion that giving the CEO anything
less than the zillion dollars rewarded to CEOs in competitive
companies (each with their own consultants) would be tanta-
mount to a vote of "no confidence." Members of the Comp
Committee are uncomfortable but keep their reservations to
themselves and go along with the seemingly "objective, scientific" findings of the consultants.

Any determined board of directors could put a stop to
this cynical game overnight. The board could simply insist on
developing its own standards, in consultation with the CEO, of
how to reward successful performance. Boards should recognize that there are two levels of CEO wealth: the wealth needed
to provide a CEO with financial security and a high-status
lifestyle, and the wealth desired mainly for scorekeeping purposes ("my bonus is bigger than yours").

The distinction is important for two reasons. One is that
the scorekeeping portion of the CEO's compensation may be

far larger than the lifestyle portion: it may involve tens of millions of dollars that the company could use for better purposes. The second reason is that these tens of millions of score-keeping dollars do not give CEOs the rewards they genuinely crave once their lifestyle needs are met. Our studies show that as the baby boomers age they are hungry for recognition and for the conviction that they are leaving a valued legacy for the future. For CEOs who are now in the boomer age range, companies are capable of providing the sort of rewards they truly value, but do not because the companies undervalue those rewards. The compensation committees of companies often act as if everything in life can be monetized: integrity, fair-mindedness, generosity of spirit, character of leadership, loyalty, breadth of vision.

In the arena of personal ego, where most CEOs dwell, what incentive do they have to take a long-term point of view when, once the CEO retires from the company, he (or she) gets scant recognition or other form of reward? The company may offer retiring CEOs an office, a secretary, and similar perks, but the typical retired CEO becomes almost a nonperson in his or her own company! If the board genuinely wants the CEO to take a long-term perspective, it should devise a range of long-term rewards that will satisfy the deep emotional needs of the CEO for recognition, legacy, and validation of performance. Under the rules of stewardship ethics, the Comp Committee should expand its definition of CEO rewards to include these kinds of intangible awards in addition to money.

If forced to choose between bigger financial benefits over and above their lifestyle aspirations, or greater respect, recognition of creative achievement, and validation of their stewardship, what would most CEOs choose? I believe most would choose recognition for high achievement. Even Enron's former

CEO Jeff Skilling, a hard-boiled executive who always presented an unruffled outward appearance to the world, came unglued when he saw all that he had worked for threatened with collapse and scandal.[8]

The success of the company is the CEO's greatest creative achievement. Added wealth is valued only to the extent that it validates that achievement—it can never substitute for it. The human ego is not built that way. Potentially, stewardship ethics can provide a far more direct validation of creative achievement than shareholder value, because it identifies and honors the CEO as a leader with integrity and breadth of concern.

Abandon or Blur?

The present situation poses a key strategic question for executives who now endorse shareholder value but are concerned about its debasement. Should they stay with the doctrine that the company's primary allegiance should be to its shareholders, however transient and speculation-driven they may be? Should they revise the methods of implementing shareholder value—for example, by linking executive rewards to longer-term performance? Or should they junk the shareholder primacy doctrine altogether? These are not easy questions.

I suspect that companies will gradually shift away from giving shareholders top priority for two weighty reasons. One is that so many shareholders are short-term. The business leader Pete Peterson points out that in some markets the turnover of a company's stock is more than 100 percent a year. "Why does it make sense," Peterson asks, "to focus on the Warren Buffett type of owner if the vast majority of the shareholders are short-term?"[9]

The second reason is that the effort to give shareholders priority distracts CEOs from their most difficult task, which is to balance competing interests. The former Meredith Corporation CEO Robert Burnett puts the point cogently:

> It is my strong belief that the corporate culture must embody the "everyone wins" commitment. All constituencies—customers, employees, shareholders, management, and the long-range responsibility to our long-range environmental (social and political) arena—must be acknowledged and served. This is a fundamental requirement, even though all constituency needs cannot be met simultaneously.[10]

The issues raised by shareholder value were addressed at a special meeting of senior executives from major global companies, convened by my firm, Viewpoint Learning. The meeting focused on how to make trust a competitive asset in the current climate of mistrust. From the outset, these executives recognized that the shareholder-value framework had delivered some benefits in productivity, efficiency, and innovation but had also narrowed the focus of business to short-term fluctuations of the stock market, away from the creation of real value.

Over two days of strategic dialogue, as they compared their own experiences, the executives concluded that shareholder value had come to mean something quite different from its initial intent and that it had become a lightning rod for public mistrust of business. Increasingly the public understands shareholder value to mean that a small group of insiders win and everyone else—including small shareholders and employees—loses. So not only does the concept have negative unanticipated consequences (distracting business from real value creation), but the term itself has reinforced public mistrust of business.

The executives considered the suggestion, made by advocates of CSR, that shareholder value be replaced by the doctrine of "stakeholder value," which argues that maximizing value for a wide range of stakeholders will lead to the long-term survival and success of a firm. They concluded that this approach for business is impractical because it provides no basis on which to set priorities and make necessary trade-offs.

Another suggestion was to adopt a concept recommended by Michael Jensen, one of the originators of the current concept of shareholder value. This is a concept of "enlightened shareholder value," which focuses on real long-term value creation and maximization.[11] The executives recognized that Jensen's revisions called for new metrics and reward systems for long-term value creation.

Whatever semantics are eventually adopted, the executives at the meeting concluded that moving away from the current short-term interpretation of shareholder value would lead to better metrics to guide business activity, to rebuild public trust, and to reach a better understanding of the value-creating role of business in society.[12]

My own judgment is that most companies would be better off in the long run if they abandoned the doctrine of shareholder value, however much they may endorse its original intent. It interacts destructively with some of the worst features of our culture. It is made to order for the Chainsaw Als of this world, who seize upon it to give an aura of legitimacy to blatantly unethical actions. (The shareholders who effectively "own" the company are precisely the fat cats that Dunlap correctly observes should *not* be the beneficiaries of shareholder value.) For every positive outcome of shareholder value, there are so many more debased outcomes that it makes one wonder whether it can ever be free of the taint of scandal, misuse, and corruption. Quite simply, shareholder value carries too much baggage to be worth salvaging.

Further, I believe that the doctrine of stewardship ethics accomplishes the same intent as shareholder value but works better in practical terms. Stewardship ethics serves the purpose of aligning the interests of shareholders with management's commitment to improve the long-term performance and value of the company. Its practical applications are less likely to be perverted and debased and more likely to achieve value for customers, employees, and the society at large. Moreover, it will do so without excessive baggage and at a higher level of corporate ethics than generally prevails in today's business sector.

IX
Restoring Gatekeeper Integrity

Deregulation—the outlook that assumes that the market works best when free of constraints—reinforces the harmful effects of shareholder value in its perverted form. The decade of the 1990s was one of the most aggressive periods of deregulation in the history of our market economy. Political conservatives, and even some liberals, pushed hard for looser, less stringent forms of regulation. Conservatives regard deregulation as part of a coherent set of ideological values. They correlate freedom from regulation with democracy, political freedom, and individualism. But conservatives were not alone. In the 1980s and 1990s, liberal economists (for example, Fred Kahn) were also arguing that heavily regulated industries like the airlines would function more efficiently with less regulation. The political pressures to deregulate met little effective opposition.

How deregulation contributed to the scandals is quite clear. Deregulation had its most direct impact on the gatekeepers—the banks, brokerages, auditors, law firms, regulatory agencies, and other entities whose purpose was, in part, to prevent these sorts of scandals from happening. It is useful to keep in mind that the majority of scandals feature accounting irregularities—cooking the books. Manipulating a company's finances for personal gain is not a new trick. It is as old as prostitution. It is one reason why the expensive, time-consuming process of having outside certified experts do financial audits of the books was invented. For many years, the nation's accounting firms earned their livelihood mainly through legally mandated audits of publicly owned corporations.

The new wave of deregulation permitted banks to get into businesses forbidden to them by the regulatory provisions of the 1933 Glass-Steagall law. It also permitted accounting firms to take on lucrative consulting assignments from the same companies for whom they were conducting audits. This deregulation immediately plunged the accounting firms into conflicts of interest, some so serious (as in the case of Arthur Andersen's involvement with Enron's finances) that they led eventually to the accounting firms' demise.

Consulting services are usually more profitable than auditing services. Accounting firms are loath to put their consulting assignments at risk by being too stiff-necked and thorough in their auditing work. The very rationale for audits—to verify the integrity of the accounts of the company—is undermined by placing too many lucrative temptations in the path of the firms charged with doing the audits. In countless ways deregulation defanged the corporate watchdogs, thereby removing one of the main safeguards that might have prevented the scandals.

Struggling with the pros and cons of regulating market economies has a long history. Since the "dark, satanic mills" of newly industrialized nineteenth-century Britain, capitalist societies have made one change after another in order to fine-tune the workings of market economies (for example, regulat-

ing hours of work and child labor). Most societies have managed to avoid extreme laissez-faire ideologies in favor of pragmatic tinkering. Many reforms have succeeded so well that cen-
tralized regulated economies have lost credibility while those
based on deft regulation supporting the goals of free markets
are spreading throughout the globe. Political leaders on the
moderate left, like Britain's Tony Blair, have learned the important lesson that the market is "too good to leave to conservatives." As an efficient method of allocating resources, the
market can easily be made to serve the purposes of those in the
center and on the moderate left of the political spectrum as
well as those on the right.

This hard-won economic consensus also helps to advance democracy as the political system most compatible with
free-market economies. But the process of regulatory fine-
tuning is far from over. The spate of recent scandals demonstrates that much additional fine-tuning is needed if market
economies are to maintain their credibility and their momentum, especially if they take on new social responsibilities.

Settling on the right kinds of regulation for business is not
easy, however. It turns out to be a complex and highly politicized
process. Everywhere you look you find ideological and political
tensions—between shareholders and management, large shareholders and small ones, shareholders and other stakeholders,
managers seeking greater freedom of action and interest groups
who want to restrict their freedom, boards of directors who
want to preserve the status quo and investors who want more
control over selecting board members, conservatives who want
to adhere to strict laissez-faire principles and liberals who want
to use the economy to support the welfare state.

A vast academic literature, full of controversy, has grown
up on the subject of corporate governance and how best to re-

solve these conflicting tensions. Considerable scholarship has been devoted to how corporate governance varies from country to country and from culture to culture. I can think of no way to keep this book short and also do justice to this extensive and thoughtful body of work. Fortunately, my position is simple enough and sufficiently limited in scope that it does not require me to do so. I am not making an ideological argument either for or against regulation, nor am I trying to specify what kinds of regulations may be needed. My focus is on the norms that are best suited to support the right sorts of regulation, whatever these may be. My position is that moving to the next stage of market capitalism requires both sound regulations and norms, each undergirding the other, and that the norms should take the form of what I have been calling stewardship ethics. I also believe that we should not depend on regulation to do the work that social norms should do.

Clearly, stewardship ethics needs some degree of legal/regulatory support, as do all normative systems. When the law and social norms fight each other, they cancel each other out. Only when they work in harmony do they make transformation possible. I personally share the business-mainstream point of view that it is better to err on the side of less rather than more regulation. An overregulated business environment implies a tendency to replace ethical norms with laws, often leading to perverse unintended consequences.

This is surely the case with the current wave of scandals. They were abetted not only by deregulation but also by the wrong kinds of regulation—regulation inappropriately designed to substitute for ethical norms. Consider, for example, the 1993 regulation that Congress designed to prevent corporations from overpaying corporate executives. The regulation placed a $1 million cap on cash salaries and bonuses by taxing the company for money it gave to its executives beyond that limit. The former CEO of Ecolab Sandy Grieves states that the regulation pushed companies into elaborate bonus schemes and options, which he cites as yet another example of unintended consequences.[1]

This $1 million cap backfired in a spectacular way. It led companies to give their executives fixed-price stock options instead of cash. In the stock market boom that followed, many executives were able to parlay these options into outsized compensation packages worth tens of millions of dollars, irrespective of how well the executives actually performed their jobs.

Nothing contributed more to the mistrust that accompanied the scandals. Americans saw this uncoupling of pay from performance (executives enriching themselves while the company and its employees lost out) as grossly unfair. Unlike some other cultures, Americans harbor little class resentment toward the huge rewards that our society gives to star performers, be they in sports, entertainment, or business. But when these rewards go to people who don't deserve them, especially when they come at the expense of hardworking employees, Americans feel anger and bitter resentment.

This is also the position taken by Peter G. Peterson, one of the nation's outstanding business leaders. Peterson served as cochairman of the Commission on Public Trust and Private Enterprise convened in 2002 by the Conference Board, a prominent business research organization. The purpose of the commission was to dig into the causes of the business scandals and to make "best-practice suggestions" for corporate governance, auditing, and executive compensation.

Peterson drafted a "personal postscript" to the commission's report that I find more pungent and compelling than the report itself, because it reflects the long personal experience of a thoughtful leader. It does not diverge widely from the official report, but it has the tone and voice of a man who has never forgotten that he is the son of poor Greek immigrants, personifying the American Dream of growing up in a society that places no limits on those with the drive, ambition, and smarts to scale to whatever heights they aspire to. Along with several other business leaders (like G.E. CEO Jeff Immelt, Starbucks' founder and chairman Howard Schultz, Procter and Gamble chairman A. G. Lafley and former chairman John Pepper, and Harman International chairman Sidney Harman), Pete Peterson personifies the stewardship ethics approach to business that I am urging in this book.

Peterson's observations are directly germane to the important issue of striking the right balance between social norms and regulation. He recognizes the importance of being very careful about what you regulate and doing it in a way that supports ethical norms instead of undercutting them.

Peterson's Postscript

On executive compensation, Peterson states that "excessive compensation was perhaps the major contributor to the dramatic loss of confidence in the governance of America's publicly held corporations." He adds that the more he delved into the issue, the more convinced he became that the main source of the public's mistrust of business was "the highly publicized reports of excessive and . . . egregious compensation of CEOs in *failing or failed companies*."[2]

Reflecting on the commission's study and analysis, he makes several recommendations consonant with a stewardship ethics approach. One is to reward executives not only on the fortunes of the stock market but also on actual performance-based operating incentives, such as improvements in return on equity, cost control, revenue growth, profit growth, and so on. With respect to corporate stock, Peterson stresses the need to shift from a short-term to a long-term orientation. He would greatly extend the holding period before a CEO could sell his or her stock, and he would tie stock incentives to the long-term success of the company, on the sound historical basis that the stock market does a better job in reflecting a company's operating success over the long term than it does in the short run.

To ensure objective implementation, he suggests that only independent directors be appointed to the compensation committees of corporate boards and that they, not management, hire and fire all consultants who deal with compensation. He cites the French philosopher René Descartes, who hundreds of years ago observed, "A man is incapable of comprehending any argument that interferes with his revenue."

On corporate governance, Peterson focuses on an area that I regard as essential to the success of stewardship ethics—the relationship of the company's CEO to its board of directors. As I shall elaborate in the next chapter, I regard this nexus as the key to overall corporate success. The relationship has to be based on the autonomy, authority, and good faith of the board. If an imperial CEO picks the board members, if they are beholden to him or her, if the CEO controls the agenda, controls the flow of information, and limits the opportunity for directors to discuss controversial issues, then the balance of power is skewed so badly toward the CEO that boards cannot carry out their responsibilities in good faith and judgment. I have served on boards where CEOs "manage" their board meetings in control-freak mode, and the system does not work as it should.

Peterson and the commission discuss a range of possible ways to open up the process for deciding which issues should be discussed at board meetings and how to ensure that they are discussed openly and frankly. All feature an independent lead director or non-CEO chairman who can guarantee the autonomy of the board and its freedom to deal with touchy issues before they reach the crisis stage. Peterson is correct in observing that this aspect of corporate governance is at the very earliest stages of evolution. He concludes: "The one indispensable element in any revised governance structure is to have one independent director . . . designated to take the lead."[3]

It may well be that there is no process solution to this core issue of corporate governance, only an ethical solution. Peterson implicitly recognizes this in his plea that when picking CEOs, boards of directors should put "character and integrity at the top of the 'must' job specifications." He concludes: "Neither technical compliance with laws, rules and regulations, nor best practices and processes would have prevented the recent scandals. Nothing is more important than tone at the top."[4]

The Role of Gatekeepers

The changes needed to stop the scandals must not only target the compensation policies and corporate governance of individual companies, they must also include changes required of the gatekeepers of business—not only government regulators but also institutional investors, auditors, business lawyers, investment bankers, business journalists, and educators. In 2005, several years after the Conference Board report, the American Academy of Arts and Sciences published a helpful and constructive series of recommendations for the gatekeepers of corporate behavior.

The report of the Academy's Corporate Responsibility Steering Committee starts out by observing, "Just as the Depression ushered in a period of intense reform, recent scandals have produced the Sarbanes-Oxley Act of 2002, new rules at the stock exchanges, a more vigilant Securities and Exchange Commission, and reenergized state attorneys general." The committee concurs with my position that corporate management has the main responsibility for correcting corporate misconduct but points out that the failures are not confined to companies and their boards but also involve clear-cut failure on the part of the gatekeepers as well. The members of the committee conclude that in the recent spate of scandals the gatekeepers compromised the values of their professions in pursuit of their own financial self-interest and that "the failure of ... gatekeepers was a recurrent theme in the business scandals." In effect, they state, the scandals represent a double failure: "The managers failed; and then the gatekeepers failed as well." The committee concludes: "The number and magnitude of corporate wrongdoing cases would have been almost inconceivable had these professionals behaved consistently with their traditional roles and the public's legitimate expectations."[5]

This harsh judgment is almost surely correct. If the gatekeepers acted as watchdogs instead of enablers, the scandals might have been confined to a few bad apples, as most businesspeople would like to believe, instead of being so widespread. I recommend the academy's report to interested readers, and although the role of gatekeepers lies outside the scope of this book, here for the sake of completeness is a brief summary of the committee's recommendations:

- For regulators, the committee recommends greater SEC independence, assured through more generous and adequate funding; special efforts by the SEC and other regulators to educate and indoctrinate managers and investors with revitalized standards of conduct (as a priority equal in importance to enforcement, inspection, and disclosure review); and a revitalized role for the stock exchanges to insist upon vigorous standards of governance.

- For institutional investors, the committee recommends that they start taking their proxy voting responsibilities seriously and stop automatically supporting management (and proxy advisory services). More important, the committee proposes that these powerful investors pressure management into focusing more on long-term strategic corporate goals and less on the short-term price of their stock.

- For the legal profession, the committee recommends the important shift in the culture of the profession away from lawyers as zealous advocates for current management to the quite different role of truly independent counsel to the company itself (as distinct from its current management). The committee stresses that lawyers owe "a public duty to the law itself" in addition to loyalty to the client. The committee faults current compensation arrangements as leading to inevitable conflicts of interests, and urges fee arrangements that encourage rather than undermine lawyers' independence.

- For auditors, the committee finds a clear deterioration of professional standards and faults the extreme concentration of auditors in a tiny number of firms. If the corporate culture of any one of these firms is corrupt, the entire profession is implicated. The committee calls on the profession to refocus its attention on the audit function (along with some limited tax work). Further, in its "fair presentation" of the company's financial condition, the profession is urged to go beyond mere technical compliance with generally accepted accounting principles toward a principled approach that does not mislead the public.

- For investment bankers (as with lawyers), the committee recommends that the client be seen as the company itself, not its current management. The distinction is a subtle one, and difficult to implement. But it is a critical step in assuring that the long-term well-being of the company is uppermost in the minds of the gatekeepers, to discourage them from enabling current management to exploit the company and its stakeholders for their own personal gain. Investment bankers need to review their ethical obligations to the investing public as well as to the company.

- For journalists and educators, the committee stresses the importance of revitalizing ethical standards, reemphasizing the importance of objectivity, and making ethical concerns a more central part of the curriculum of business schools and of the corporate culture of individual firms. (The former Ecolab CEO Sandy Grieves points out that all the business schools where he serves as trustee have moved from giving stand-alone

courses on ethics to building ethics into every
business course.)[6]

It is noteworthy that these recommendations emphasize
renewal of ethical norms far more than legal/regulatory mechanisms. Admittedly, these are harder to implement, but that
does not mean that we should substitute regulations for them.
Our society has a rich ethical tradition on which to draw, if the
political will exists to do so.

In summary, it is useful to distinguish between the actions
needed to stop the scandals and those needed to advance market capitalism to its next stage. The two do not automatically
support each other. Our society can stop or slow the scandals
through brutal regulation and punishment without advancing
to a new style of market capitalism. And conversely, we can enhance the global impact of market capitalism without stopping the scandals. It will take consummate management skill
and goodwill to forge the two initiatives into a single coherent
strategy—one in which doing good for the economic well-
being of the world and upgrading corporate ethical standards
are accomplished at the same time. There is no more important challenge facing corporate management.

Making the two goals compatible requires deft-handed
regulation and practical social norms to work together in tan-
dem. To halt the scandals, regulation and punitive restraints
may play the bigger role, with social norms in support. But
when it comes to responding to the new global economy, the
emphasis is reversed. Here, social norms take the lead, with
support from the legal/regulatory side.

X

Hummer versus Hybrid

The global economy cries out for American business to respond to a series of daunting challenges. Domestically, the business sector is responsible for maintaining high levels of productivity, employment, capital investment, and stimulation of consumer spending. Internationally, the business community has the great responsibility—and privilege—of helping to lift the majority of the world's population out of poverty, poor health, and deprivation. Today's multinational corporations, with their powerful integrations of capital, technology, and managerial skills, constitute just about the only force capable of transforming billions of people subsisting on meager incomes of one or two dollars a day into active participants in thriving market economies.

But our corporations cannot perform these outstanding deeds without enlightened policies and public goodwill. Scandals eat away at that goodwill like maggots. Instead of basking in the warmth of public approval and respect, the leaders of our corporations are seen as greedy opportunists seeking to enrich themselves at the expense of their employees, customers, and the general public.

In the previous chapter I described some of the reforms needed in the role of gatekeepers. Gatekeepers are important. But in the final analysis, it is the CEOs and boards of individual corporations who hold the key to stopping the scandals. Only they can restore the climate of confidence and trust that business needs if it is to move onto a new stage of market capitalism. As the American Academy's Corporate Responsibility Committee acknowledges, if scandals are to be limited to a few rogue companies, the major responsibility for reform depends on the actions of individual companies—the focus of this book.[1] At the level of individual companies, there are as yet few signs of dramatic change and reform. In my view, reform will come gradually and undramatically. It may even be imperceptible, but it will surely come.

Reforms will probably begin in the boardrooms of companies whose stock has fallen from favor because of the scandals. In corporate retreats, thoughtful directors and company executives will begin to design new incentive programs that align the company's interests not only with those of shareholders and with short-term goals but also with its long-term strategic goals, as well as with the interests of customers, employees, and the community. This is a first step toward stewardship ethics.

Companies tainted by scandal must accept the reality that restoring their reputation is a priority that they cannot shirk. Their boards cannot responsibly let them do otherwise. At the same time, companies untainted by scandal are starting to recognize the great competitive advantage they can reap by strengthening their reputations for integrity and good stewardship.

In other words, the lessons learned from recent experience with the scandals are just beginning to be applied. Their effects are not yet robust or positive enough to dispel the climate of mistrust and stop further scandals. More fundamental rethinking is called for. But by giving business a positive incentive to move to a higher standard of ethical performance—the level of stewardship ethics—the scandals give businesses an opportunity to transform a liability into an asset.

Before discussing the tactics to achieve this goal—the subject of this final chapter—it may be useful to recap the core meanings of stewardship ethics in relationship to our democratic form of government.

Core Meanings

In earlier chapters I identified these key attributes:

- ✓ Stewardship ethics always involves selectivity and caring—selecting those whom the company cares for and how it expresses that caring.
- ✓ Stewardship ethics emphasizes the community side of the corporation—the need to develop communal values.
- ✓ Stewardship ethics always seeks to leave the institution better off than it was when the CEO's stewardship began.
- ✓ Stewardship ethics responds positively to the society's insistence that more is expected of those with substantial resources and economic power.
- ✓ Stewardship ethics emphasizes the conscious effort required to reconcile profitability with social good.

A number of companies are moving in this direction. Starbucks gives special care to its suppliers, its coffee growers. Southwest Airlines is clear about its selectivity: its president has been quoted as saying, "We have the pyramid upside down. Employees are first. Passengers are second. Shareholders are third."[2] Procter and Gamble regards the community side of the business as an essential part of its core values. The former CEO John Pepper writes: "I believe being a community is Procter and Gamble's greatest competitive advantage."[3] High among Hewlett-Packard's core values is the belief that the company exists to make technical contributions that will benefit society and not just make money. G.E. is making a conscious effort to reconcile profitability with using new technology to meet pressing environmental needs. As Dell became a leader in the computer industry, it faced ever-greater pressures to take the lead in recycling, and now Dell treats recycling as a profit center.

Stewardship ethics is a contemporary form of enlightened self-interest. The question all corporate management must answer is: "What is the best way for our company to pursue its enlightened self-interest at this particular time and under the changing conditions under which we operate?"

The focus on enlightened self-interest makes this a very traditional question. The focus on changing conditions makes it a contemporary question. Posing the question as one requiring a thoughtful, serious empirical answer presupposes a pragmatic approach rather than an ideological one.

The question makes these assumptions about a company's enlightened self-interest:

1. It will differ from company to company and industry to industry
2. It is likely to change as circumstances change
3. It will require a special effort on behalf of the company to align its interests with those of the larger society.

It is this third assumption that will cause controversy. Unlike classic laissez-faire doctrine, stewardship ethics does not presuppose that all reasonably honest ways of making profit somehow serve the public good. There are simply too many instances of "market failure" in which the pursuit of profit comes at the expense of the public interest rather than advancing it.

Pragmatists will recognize that the traditional what's-good-for-business-is-good-for-the-country ideology is sometimes correct and sometimes incorrect. As corporations take a closer look at the link between their profit-making strategies and their obligations to take care of a variety of constituencies, they will see that some profit-making strategies do not benefit stakeholders they care about—or should care about.

Wal-Mart's lower prices, for instance, may well come at the expense of its one million employees. Detroit's love affair with SUV profits may come at the expense of the nation's energy independence. By remaining in denial about the nation's need for greater fuel efficiency, Detroit's automobile manufacturers have defined their self-interest in ways that pit it against the common interest. Big pharma's habit of demanding huge price hikes for marginal improvements in existing drugs comes at the expense of hard-pressed consumers and the public at large. In all these instances, self-interest is *un*enlightened because it is not aligned with the interests of the society.

The most creative challenge of stewardship ethics is to learn how to make profitability and society's interests more compatible. A company can, for example, pursue environmental policies in ways that undermine either its own profits or the environment, or it can develop strategies toward the environment that make profits and sustainability compatible. A number of the world's largest oil companies are finding new ways to reconcile the search for sustainability with profitability. A billionaire real estate developer in Syracuse, New York, Robert Congel, has found imaginative new ways to rescue the city's most blighted areas to everyone's benefit. G.E. has organized a program that it calls Ecomagination to apply new technologies to solve environmental problems. Under Ecomagination, G.E. plans to more than double its research and development from $700 million a year in 2004 to $1.5 billion in the coming years. Upon launching the new program, G.E. CEO Jeff Immelt said: "Ecomagination is G.E.'s commitment to address challenges such as the need for cleaner, more efficient sources of energy, reduced emissions and abundant sources of clean water. And we plan to make money doing it. Increasingly for business, 'green is green.'" It is just as blind to assume that companies cannot pursue profit making while also seeking to do good as it is to assume that all forms of profit seeking automatically result in social good.[4]

The Link to Democracy

Consider a controversial example of the search for enlightened self-interest. Many observers believe that by flooding the housing market with risky new interest-only and adjustable-rate mortgages, the nation's banks may be creating a housing bubble, thereby undermining the public interest. If true, the banks would be guilty of *un*enlightened self-interest.

The banks argue strenuously against this widespread assumption. They cite Alan Greenspan's statement that "the traditional mortgage may be an expensive method of financing a home." They argue that the new mortgages do not contribute to a housing bubble, that on the contrary, they advance the American Dream of home ownership while adding to bank profits.[5]

Time will prove who is right and wrong in this debate. The point is that identifying true enlightened self-interest is often difficult and controversial.

It is this difficulty that makes the link between steward-ship ethics and democracy compelling. The search always involves a jumble of competing interests and judgments. Having all of the varied interests compete in a democratic fashion, with all participants having a voice, is probably the only practical way the system can work. Expert advice may be needed for technical input, but the most important decisions always involve values and interests, and there is no satisfactory alternative to democracy to settle the clash of values and interests.

Why must companies such as mortgage lending banks actively seek to align their interests with the common interest? Why shouldn't privately owned companies go about their business of maximizing their profits without regard to responsibilities that are properly those of government? The general public elects public officials; they do not elect CEOs, who are not accountable to them.

Fortunately, our democracy encourages enlightened self-interest by creating checks and balances that make the system self-corrective. If the banks are proven correct, their reputation will be enhanced. If they are proven wrong, not only will their reputation suffer, but the voting public will demand regulation that imposes new constraints on them, some punitive in character.

In a democracy, reputation is all-important. The reputation of a company and its associated brand names may be a company's most valuable asset—and all thoughtful business executives realize this. The care and feeding of the company's reputation is a vital aspect of the CEO's responsibilities. Operationally, reputation reflects how well the company meets the expectations of various stakeholders (including the voting public). If and when a company is able to gain a superior reputation by meeting or exceeding these expectations, it enjoys a sizable edge over its competitors. For fallen angels like Merck and Shell, a loss of reputation is a serious blow, and these companies' efforts to regain their good name must be unremitting.

Tactics

Implementing stewardship ethics confronts companies with a number of vital tactical issues:

- If a company adopts a longer time perspective, how can it avoid a huge hit to the short-term price of its stock?
- How should the company deal with the demands of employees, customers, environmentalists, and the larger community if and when these conflict with shareholder interests?
- How can the company upgrade the ethical tone of its corporate culture when the culture of the larger society appears to be working against it?
- How can the company systematically reconcile its profitability goals with a commitment to advance overall social welfare?
- What is the best way for the company to effect a transition from shareholder value to stewardship ethics?

I will discuss these questions individually; however, one general answer applies to all of them. In each case the nexus between the CEO and the board of directors is the key to success.

Every company that enjoys a healthy, mutually trusting relationship between CEO and board follows a process that constantly reinforces the bond of trust. The CEO submits proposals for policy changes to the board (some offered by board members), and the board deliberates by engaging the CEO in the kind of dialogue that leads to the company's most important decisions.

CEOs must accept the responsibility not only for executing policy but also for originating it. A typical board of directors meets four to ten times a year for a half-day or a day, occasionally supplemented with a board retreat when considering exceptional policy shifts. The board is therefore directly engaged in the company's business no more than a dozen full days a year, hardly enough time to learn how to manage the company. If the CEO does not perform to expectations, the board has only one recourse, which is to find itself a new CEO. But until replaced, the CEO runs the company, makes the hard calls, and frames key decisions for board deliberation.

What CEOs need most from their boards is thoughtful collective judgment. The board must serve as a genuine "sounding board" for testing the CEO's best ideas (the worst ones should be killed off before the board meets). What boards require of their CEOs is greater openness. All too often in recent years the board's trust in its CEO has been misplaced.

Consider the first question above—how to avoid getting your stock pummeled if your company wants to shift to a longer time horizon. Sometimes taking the longer view puts the profits of the next few quarters or even the next couple of years at risk. This question holds particular urgency for a board of directors in its role as representative of the company's shareholders.

Let us imagine that a CEO proposes changes in company policy that he realizes may hurt the price of the stock in the short run, even though the changes promise to improve long-term profitability. He prepares himself to review these changes at the next board meeting. He knows that he has a lot of homework to do. He realizes that the board will not consider confronting—and disappointing—Wall Street with a negative surprise about short-term earnings unless he can demonstrate significant long-term benefits for the company. If the board agrees that his proposals are sound, its questions will then shift to tactics of implementation. Boards, more than company executives, are predisposed to favor decisions that strengthen the long-term health of the company—because that is where the true interests of stakeholders lie. If the CEO is not convincing, he risks failure in winning the board's approval and, in extreme cases, losing his job. (Carly Fiorina at Hewlett-Packard is not the only one to have lived out this scenario.)

Jack McAllister, a former US West CEO, writes, "During my tenure this issue came up frequently, as in the case of the introduction of cellular service. It required short-term losses with the promise of long-term profits. Installing fiber optics systems also carried with it short-term loss with long-term profits and service improvements."[6]

The same considerations apply to all of the tactical issues listed above. Every one of them falls within the sphere of the CEO's responsibilities and cannot be delegated to lower levels of the corporate hierarchy. Every one of them also involves active board participation and support. Success in implementing stewardship ethics in each individual company depends on the quality and strength of the CEO's relationship to the company's board of directors.

DISAPPOINTING WALL STREET EXPECTATIONS

Introducing policy changes that will cause a company to dis-
appoint Wall Street's short-term profit expectations is a brutal
ordeal for both the CEO and the board. If the company misses
Wall Street's expectations for its quarterly earnings even by
a penny or two per share, the stock will take a big hit. It may
momentarily lose from 5 percent to 25 percent of its market
value—adding up to billions of dollars for large corporations.
Short-term traders—hedge funds, momentum players, many
mutual funds—will immediately abandon the company's stock.
Some will also build up short positions in the stock, putting it
under further pressure.

In principle, there should be an ample supply of long-term
investors ready to replace the short-term traders, but they too
need to be convinced that the company is on the right path. That
can take a lot of time and require companies to climb a wall of
skepticism. Putative future profits are chancier than bird-in-
the-hand existing profits. The shift to a longer time frame adds
considerable risk for investors, especially for those who lack an
intimate knowledge of the company and its industry.

The decision to favor the longer term and abandon the
tyranny of having to produce smooth, steady, predictable,
ever-increasing earnings quarter after quarter has large consequences. At the CEO/board level, the company needs to know
what those consequences are and to feel confident that they
can be successfully managed. There are a number of ways to do
this. One is for the CEO and other key company executives to
conduct "road shows" throughout the country that give analysts and investors well-documented briefings on the sound-
ness of the business reasons for the company's decision to sacrifice short-term earnings.

The purpose of the road shows is to convert uncertainty to risk. Investors hate uncertainty but live daily with risk. If earnings falter without explanation, uncertainty—the bugaboo of Wall Street—prevails. Risk is another matter. Investors are comfortable with risk: it is the core of their work. Successful road shows replace unacceptable uncertainty with acceptable risk assessment. If the company's board of directors thinks the risk makes sense, the chances are that well-informed investors will as well. The stock will still take a short-term hit. Investors have the luxury that the board does not have of saying, "Well, I'll sell the stock and buy it back later, if they turn out to be right." In making their decision to sacrifice current profits for larger future profits, boards should assume that while the stock may momentarily go down, it will rise to far greater heights in the future—if the company's strategy is sound.

GIVING OTHER STAKEHOLDERS THEIR DUE

The doctrine that gives shareholders preference over employees, customers, the general public, and other stakeholders was not in vogue when I entered the business world in the 1950s and 1960s. On the contrary, at that time CEOs of major corporations went out of their way to state explicitly that their job was to balance the interests of all groups of important stakeholders, with shareholders counted as only one among four or five such constituencies. Giant companies like General Motors and Standard Oil of New Jersey (now Exxon-Mobil) included the national interest as one constituency, along with their customers, employees, shareholders, suppliers, and the local communities where they had business interests.

Achieving the best possible balance among all constituencies is, arguably, the CEO's most difficult assignment, far more difficult than managing the day-to-day operations of the company. Experience shows that anytime one group of stakeholders can sweep aside the interests of the others, trouble follows. Some of the economic stagnation of countries like Sweden and Germany grew out of the disproportionate influence of the labor unions in those countries. They put their own interests ahead of the interests of the general public, customers, and national economies. Eventually they dragged their economies down to levels far below their true potential.

Labor unions lost influence in the United States for similar reasons. American labor unions are organized for adversarial battle. They fight to put the interests of their members ahead of everyone else's, including the general public's. There may have been sound historical reasons for having adopting this adversarial practice, but the ill will unions now generate because of it has undermined their influence. (This is not the only reason unions have lost influence, but it is one whose importance has been underestimated.)

In our era of growing inequality, labor unions can do a lot to improve their members' lives and serve the interests of the larger society as well. (Our society functions best when inequality is kept within the limits of social justice.) But their chances for success will be much better if they abandon their deeply ingrained practice of zero-sum unenlightened self-interest in favor of searching for ways to reconcile their members' interests with those of others. Southwest Airlines, a heavily unionized company, has found ways to keep their customers happy by keeping their employees content and highly motivated. It can be done, but it will require cooperation rather than the militant tactics of the past.

Those who insist that the interests of shareholders take preference over all other stakeholders also invite a loss of influence. The day-to-day practice of this doctrine is stirring up a backlash among the general public. Fewer than three out of ten Americans believe that companies are being fair to their workers and customers.[7]

It is not necessary for business to revert to the "balance of interests" doctrine that dominated business before shareholder value came into fashion. Our world has changed beyond recognition since then, and new viewpoints are called for. Stewardship ethics dictates that a company give appropriate levels of caring to each of its important constituencies, and predicts that the caring will pay off in competitive advantage. For example, airlines like JetBlue and Southwest are taking business away from traditional carriers like United and Delta not only because their fares are lower but also because their courtesy and efficiency appeal to passengers. These new airlines have learned how to motivate employees to be friendly, courteous, and helpful to their passengers, thereby reconciling the interests of shareholders, employees, and the flying public. The older airlines think that by setting up separate low-cost airlines with cute names like Ted and Song they can undercut their new competitors. But as long as Ted, Song, and the others are staffed by demoralized, surly, indifferent, unhappy employees, they will lose the competitive struggle for customers.

It is important for a company's success that neither its employees nor its customers feel that they are being treated as second-class citizens, with their interests subordinated to those of shareholders. The company should stress that caring for its customers and employees is the best way to care for its shareholders as well. Wall Street is indifferent to a company's rhetoric and theories but cares intensely about promised profits.

Procter and Gamble is a stock market favorite because its financial success is so closely tied to its care for its employees and consumers. Procter and Gamble's dedication to employees and to consumer need is the bedrock of company policy. It is this uncompromising concern that makes Procter and Gamble a legend among marketers—and a key to their huge success. Only once did Procter and Gamble falter from this path (in the late 1990s), and the company quickly returned to what it rightly regards the core of its business. The former CEO John Pepper credits the company's ingrained principle of "preserv[ing] the core, be[ing] ready to change everything else." For Procter and Gamble serving the consumer and creating community among its employees is an essential part of that core. Procter and Gamble has learned that in the long run, this is the best way to serve shareholders.[8]

The kind of commitment that gives a company a competitive edge on employee and customer satisfaction does not happen by accident. It requires extraordinary special effort, ideally within the framework of stewardship ethics.

UPGRADING CORPORATE ETHICS

In earlier chapters, I described a "machine for scandal" created by mixing the culture of winning-for-myself with the business norms of shareholder value and deregulation. No improved set of business ethics can succeed if the larger culture does not support it. It is difficult to see how corporate endorsement of stewardship ethics can successfully take root as long as a fierce desire to win at all costs drives the mainstream of corporate executives. To the extent that the broader culture endorses this zealous preoccupation with winning at everyone else's expense, the chances are that stewardship ethics will fail. It will suffer the same fate as shareholder value—positive in promise, perverse in practice. For stewardship ethics to take hold firmly in today's corporate culture without debasement or distortion, individual self-seeking must become less ferocious. Other, more communal civil society motivations must rise to the surface. Is such a goal feasible in today's general culture, and if so, how can CEOs achieve it in practical ways?

The good news is that the larger culture is ready for less-self-centered, more-communal-minded values. In fact, corporate America has lagged behind the nation's broader culture, which is rapidly moving away from the crasser forms of self-seeking and is instead eager to see civil society norms grow stronger.[9] This is especially true in the case of those norms that I think of as the Four Cs of Civil Society:

- Caring
- Community
- Civility
- Cooperation

My firm DYG's annual tracking studies of American values (SCAN) show that in today's United States, the search is on for these more-communal ethical values. In this quest, women are largely leading the way, seeking ways to strengthen family stability, to take better care of both their children and their aging parents, to be good stewards of the environment, and in general to pay greater heed to the communal values of civil society.[10] Men have similar concerns (although at somewhat lower levels of intensity), along with a special concern for making a contribution to the larger society.

Most executives pursue these broader goals in their private lives to a greater extent than in their corporate pursuits. But they would welcome the opportunity to integrate these values into their business careers, provided they could be convinced that the two can be made compatible. Making them compatible is one of the main goals of stewardship ethics.

The CEO plays an indispensable role in setting the ethical tone of a company's corporate culture. *CEO* should stand for Chief Ethical Officer as well as Chief Executive Officer. Both inside the company and to the outside world, the CEO *is* the company. This reality sometimes creates painful dilemmas. Boeing was obliged to let its highly successful CEO Harry Stonecipher retire for a second time when it was revealed that he was having an affair with another Boeing executive. Boeing's ethical problems were unrelated to sexual mores, but the company felt it could not afford to appear hypocritical when its board had made raising the ethical tone of the company a top priority.

The main obstacle to raising ethical standards is the almost inevitable gap between rhetoric and reality. It is fatally easy to "talk the talk." Enron's CEO, Ken Lay, was a master at presenting Enron as the personification of an innovative, community-minded, highly ethical company, whereas the reality was grotesquely different. In practice, Enron's corporate culture was personified by the company's young techies hard at work at their computers, busily rigging California's energy market.

Sidney Harman, founder and executive chairman of Harman International, a manufacturer of high-end audio equipment, recounts an example of how his company demonstrated its ethical concern for its employees. After a production employee's former husband murdered her as she was leaving work, the company did more than help to care for the woman's surviving child. Recognizing that almost one-third of the country's female population suffers from domestic violence, the company organized a company-wide domestic violence program that provides professional training and security to its employees. In this way, the company seeks to create a helping and constructive environment and a feeling of community.[11]

CEOs should assume that even the company's own employees (as well as the larger community) will be skeptical of its ethical claims until the company demonstrates that it really means what it says. Typically, a climate of skepticism will prevail until a conflict arises between the company's ethics and its short-term profits, comfort, convenience, or prideful self-image. Employees will watch carefully to see what the CEO does. If he or she does the usual thing (mouthing ethical principles while practicing expediency), the corporate culture will stay in its familiar old rut, resisting change. Only if the CEO chooses the ethical course over the expedient one will people take note and begin to take the company's ethical commitments seriously.

RECONCILING PROFITABILITY WITH STEWARDSHIP ETHICS

Consider the differences between the largest sport utility vehicles like General Motors' Escalade and Hummer compared with Toyota's Prius. They symbolize the contrast between short-term profit making and stewardship ethics. The Hummer is a gas-guzzling tank for drivers who want to control the road. It is ludicrously wasteful of energy. And it makes a lot of profit for General Motors, as do all of General Motors' SUVs that are built on a truck chassis. G.M.'s vice chairman Robert Lutz admits that the big SUVs are "where the company makes, frankly, high margins." The Hummer puts the company's short-term profitability ahead of everything and everyone else, including society's well-being.[12]

The Prius hybrid falls at the other extreme of the spectrum. It is a highly economical vehicle, getting many times better mileage per gallon than the Hummer. It is moderately priced, giving good quality and value for the money. And it is a quiet, well-designed, nonbullying car. It represents a serious technological effort to alleviate our problem of energy dependence without demanding sacrifice on the part of the consumer. Toyota made no profit on its Prius in the first few years of its existence but expects to be profitable soon.

The Hummer and the Prius represent two different mindsets. One says, "Push the cars with the high margins irrespective of long-term consequences, even the future well-being of the company." The other says, "Let's use our resources to solve an important societal problem and make a profit on it."

The pharmaceutical industry is traveling the same self-defeating road as G.M. Leading drug companies complain bitterly about being lumped together with cigarette companies on the grounds that cigarette companies threaten people's health while drug companies do everything in their power to improve it. Opinion polls show that pharmaceutical company executives have a much higher opinion of their own business ethics than the public does. Almost two-thirds of the industry's executives give themselves high marks on "ethical business practices," while more than two-thirds of the public believes that the industry puts its own profits ahead of people. A majority does not trust the leadership of major pharmaceutical companies to "engage in ethical business practices."[13]

Not only are the drug companies a target for growing consumer mistrust, their stocks have steadily lost favor, losing billions of dollars in market value in recent years. And yet drug company executives have scant insight into the role they play in causing so much damage to themselves. They blame everyone but themselves. They do not grasp the reality that putting their short-term profitability goals ahead of consumer interests is a major cause of their troubles. They find it impossible to escape the prison of this limited mindset.

It never seems to occur to the pharmaceutical industry to search for ways to give consumers some relief from relentless price increases for products that are not discretionary from the consumer's point of view. They do not understand the fundamental lesson that more is expected of companies that enjoy immense privileges of power and influence. Because consumers of prescription drugs do not have a wide range of pharmaceutical choices, these companies exemplify the flaws in traditional laissez-faire ideology much more than does General Motors: consumers have plenty of choices besides Hummers and other SUVs. Many of the drug companies are blind or indifferent to their own role as exploiters of the public.

A glance at Figure 5 shows how vast a gap can exist between the stewardship expectations of the society and the company's perceived performances. The long bars measure the expectations of members of Congress and other leaders; the short bars atop them measure how well these leaders think the company—a major pipeline company—is meeting their expectations.

The chart presents a vivid statistical image of a company in deep trouble with major constituencies because of its failure to recognize and respond to heightened stewardship obligations.

HOW TO MAKE THE TRANSITION

Tactics for making the transition to stewardship ethics will vary from company to company. One way to do the hard work involved in stewardship ethics is for the company's CEO to organize a special task force inside the company that reports di-

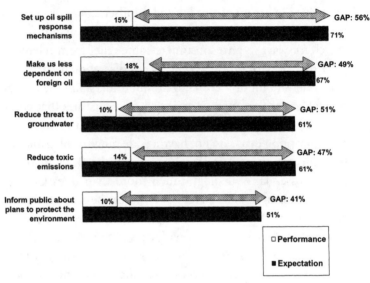

Figure 5. An example of the stewardship gap:
A pipeline company (mid-1990s)

rectly to the CEO. Companies that are serious about implementing stewardship ethics will quickly learn that they need to
form special work groups that cut across traditional lines of
organization if they are to achieve the task of reconciling the
pursuit of profitability with an expanded orbit of care for the
company's many stakeholders.

The CEO might select a small group of no more than a
dozen of the company's most thoughtful executives, from a variety of functions and divisions. They might, for example,
bring marketing executives together with engineers, scientists,
finance, and human resource executives from across the spectrum of the company's activities. The CEO might invite former CEOs (and directors) to serve in these groups.

This diverse group of people—who may never have worked together before—will be charged with the task of conducting *strategic dialogue* on how best to take advantage of changes occurring in the markets in which the company operates.[14] The "strategic" aspect of strategic dialogue relates to formulating ways the company can create new opportunities for itself through repositioning existing products or creating new products and services. The "dialogue" aspect refers to the mode of discourse that the task force adopts.

Why the stress on dialogue? The main reason is that ordinary communication methods don't work well for this purpose. The conventional meeting format works well enough for executives who happen to share the same framework—engineers talking to engineers, marketers meeting with other marketers, American executives meeting with other Americans. But when you mix people who don't share the same framework you encounter unimaginable obstacles to effective communication, especially if you want people to work together as a team to generate new strategies for the company. Try knitting together Japanese financial executives with American marketers, German engineers, and British designers as a creative team to do strategic planning for the company, and you will quickly learn that you need the special communication techniques associated with dialogue to transcend the lack of a shared framework. Yet in spite of the challenge, bringing such diverse perspectives together creates the opportunity for new insights that cannot be reached when people communicate only within a particular narrow shared framework.

Both domestically and in foreign markets, these work groups should engage the issues that are strategically vital to the company's future. How can the company strengthen its brand franchise in its home market? How can it take advantage of change to introduce new products, packaging, pricing, and service? How can it package, distribute, and price a company's products and services abroad in new low-income markets? How can it help change long-standing financial practices (like redlining or restrictive lending practices) that both make poverty more entrenched and limit the company's opportunities? How can it provide management with the right incentives to take a long-term perspective when Wall Street is focused on short-term results and when the primary rewards for a long-term approach will be reaped not by the CEO but by his or her successors?

These are questions that require serious deliberation and a high level of strategic thinking. The company's strategic work teams become the CEO's instrument for shaping decisions for board consideration about how to make profits while at the same time advancing the well-being of employees, consumers, and the larger society.

All of the tactics for implementing stewardship ethics point in the same direction: CEO leadership with strong board support. The ethical renewal of the nation's business sector will not, in my view, come about as a result of throwing a few executive con men in jail or passing a slew of new punitive laws. Nor will it come from moral exhortations to business from social movements with roots outside the business community.

I am not arguing against these efforts. They are important, and may be necessary. But they are surely not sufficient. The major initiative must come from within the business sector itself. And it must come company by company, led by individual CEOs who become convinced that stewardship ethics will give them a strategic competitive advantage in the marketplace and who know how to use their boards for the judgment, support, and validation they need to implement their policies. And it will provide success models for other companies to emulate.

This is an optimistic conclusion. It is a bet on stewardship ethics to become the legitimate successor to shareholder value, along with the more thoughtful forms of CSR. Within any one company, making the shift depends on the mindset, determination, and leadership of a tiny number of people—no more than fifteen to twenty. If they decide it will be in the best interests of the company to make the change, they have the power, the influence, the knowledge, and the skill to bring it about. If they do so, others will follow. In our culture, where events move so quickly, the transformation to stewardship ethics may take place without even being widely noticed. But its effects will register in enhanced trust in the business sector, in improved long-term profitability, and in significant advances in global well-being.

Appendix

Daniel Yankelovich's Directorships and Trusteeships

Arkla, Inc.
Brown University
Carnegie Foundation for the Advancement of
    Education
CBS, Inc.
The Concord Coalition
Diversified Energies, Inc.
DYG, Inc. (cofounder; chairman of the board)
Educational Testing Service (chairman of the
    board)
Fund for the City of New York
The Japan Society
The Charles F. Kettering Foundation
Loral Space and Communications Corporation
Meredith Corporation (chairman of the Pension
    Committee)
Minnegasco, Inc.
The Public Agenda (cofounder with Cyrus Vance;
    chairman of the board)

Reliance Group, Inc.

Society for the Advancement of Socio-Economics
(president, 1992–1993)

Sunmark Industries, Inc.

US West, Inc. (chairman of the Investment Committee)

Viewpoint Learning, Inc. (founder; chairman of
the board)

Yankelovich, Skelly and White, Inc. (founder;
chairman of the board)

Notes

Introduction

1. Gourevitch and Shinn, *Political Power and Corporate Control*, introduction.

2. Berle and Means, *Modern Corporation and Private Property*, 122.

3. Heilbroner, *21st Century Capitalism*, 53–57.

4. Jackson and Nelson, *Profits with Principles*, 244.

5. See Kotler and Lee, *Corporate Social Responsibility*, 8–10.

6. See, for example, Robert Heilbroner's *21st Century Capitalism* and Niall Ferguson's *Colossus*.

7. See Public Agenda, *For Goodness' Sake*, chapter 1.

8. In an August 2005 *Newsweek* poll, only 36 percent were "satisfied with the way things are going in the United States at this time." Similarly, in an AP/Ipsos poll in the same time period, only 37 percent felt that "things in this country are heading in the right direction."

9. Quoted in Pepper, *What Really Matters*, 289.

1. The Wrong Way to Stop the Scandals

1. *Wall Street Week with Fortune*. Aired on PBS, December 24, 2004.

2. Screwed Again

1. DYG SCAN annual survey 2002, DYG, Inc., Danbury, Connecticut. Other surveys have produced similar findings.

3. *Un*enlightened Self-Interest

1. Eichenwald, "Reform Effort."
2. Ibid.
3. *Wall Street Journal,* September 10, 2002.
4. See Gourevitch and Shinn, *Political Power and Corporate Control.*

4. Yesterday's versus Today's Ethical Norms

1. Due to a change in editorship, the results were never published in the *Review.*
2. I discuss this phenomenon extensively in *New Rules.*
3. The Yankelovich Monitor and DYG's SCAN.
4. See Yankelovich, *New Rules.*
5. DYG SCAN 2004.

5. Two Incomplete Visions

1. Schwartz and Leyden, "Long Boom," 116, 168–71.
2. Personal communication.
3. Yankelovich, *The Magic of Dialogue,* 213–14.

6. Unpacking Stewardship Ethics

1. Mary Williams Walsh, "How Wall Street Wrecked United's Pension," *New York Times,* July 31, 2005.
2. Thomas Friedman, "Learning from Lance," *New York Times,* July 27, 2005.
3. Crook, "Good Company."
4. Ibid.
5. Pepper, *What Really Matters.*
6. Garfinkle, "Future of the American Dream."
7. Boyle, "The 100 Best Companies to Work For," *Fortune,* January 24, 2005.
8. Shellenberger and Nordhaus, "Death of Environmentalism," 32–34.

7. The Vision of Stewardship Ethics

1. *Wall Street Journal,* February 25, 2005.
2. Crook, "Good Company."

3. Yankelovich, "Corporate Logic in the 1990s," 7.

4. Yankelovich, Skelly and White Poll 1982; Gallup Poll 2002.

5. Ibid.

6. Pepper, *What Really Matters,* 198–99.

8. What to Do about Shareholder Value

1. Cassidy, "Greed Cycle," 64.

2. Eisinger, "Follow the CEO's Money."

3. Floyd Norris, "Stock Options: Do They Make Bosses Cheat?" *New York Times,* August 5, 2005.

4. Personal communication.

5. Cassidy, "Greed Cycle," 64.

6. Quoted in Rakesh Khurana, Nitin Nohria, and Daniel Penrice, "Management as a Profession," in Lorsch et al., *Restoring Trust,* 43–60.

7. Margaret Blair, "Should Directors Be Professionals?" in Lorsch et al., *Restoring Trust,* 79–83.

8. See Eichenwald, *Conspiracy of Fools.*

9. Personal communication.

10. Personal communication.

11. Jensen, "Value Maximization."

12. For a summary report of the conclusions reached at this special meeting of senior executives, see Yankelovich and Rosell, *Making Trust a Competitive Asset: Breaking Out of Narrow Frameworks.*

9. Restoring Gatekeeper Integrity

1. Personal communication.

2. Peterson, "Personal Postscript," 7 (emphasis in original)

3. Ibid., 15.

4. Ibid., 16.

5. Lorsch et al., *Restoring Trust,* 161–76.

6. Personal communication.

10. Hummer versus Hybrid

1. Lorsch, et al., *Restoring Trust,* 161–76.

2. Gunther, *Faith and Fortune,* 75.

3. Pepper, *What Really Matters,* 10.

4. Personal communication from Dr. Charles Kennel, director, Scripps Institute of Oceanography, UCSD; G.E. press release, May 9, 2005.

5. See Neil Barsky, "What Housing Bubble?" *Wall Street Journal*, July 28, 2005.

6. Personal communication.

7. DYG SCAN, 2004.

8. Pepper, *What Really Matters*.

9. DYG SCAN 2003, 2004.

10. Ibid.

11. Personal communication.

12. Hakim, "G.M. to Seek Cuts." Loopholes in federal law that exempt SUVs built on truck chassis from clean-air and mileage standards that apply to passenger cars, while also allowing large tax write-offs for consumers who purchase them for "business purposes," only add insult to injury. See Bradsher, *High and Mighty*.

13. Roner, "U.S. Pharmaceutical Ethics," 1.

14. For additional information on strategic dialogue, see Daniel Yankelovich and Steven Rosell, "Creating Strategic Dialogue," in *The Financial Times Handbook of Management*, 3rd ed., eds. Stuart Crainer and Des Dearlove (Prentice Hall: 2004), 851–55. A description of the Strategic Dialogue method can also be found at www.ViewpointLearning.com/lprogramsfs.html.

Bibliography

Albert, Michel. *Capitalism vs. Capitalism: How America's Obsession with Individual Achievement and Short-term Profit Has Led It to the Brink of Collapse.* New York: Four Walls Eight Windows, 1993.

Belson, Ken. "WorldCom's Audacious Failure and Its Toll on an Industry." *New York Times,* January 18, 2005.

Berle, Adolf A., and Gardiner C. Means. *The Modern Corporation and Private Property.* New York: Harcourt, Brace and World, 1932.

Bossidy, Larry, and Ram Charan. *Execution: The Discipline of Getting Things Done.* New York: Crown Business, 2002.

Boyle, Matthew. "The 100 Best Companies to Work For: The Wegman's Way." *Fortune,* January 24, 2005.

Bradsher, Keith. *High and Mighty: SUVs, The World's Most Dangerous Vehicles and How They Got That Way.* New York: PublicAffairs, 2002.

Cassidy, John. "The Greed Cycle: How the Financial System Encouraged Corporations to Go Crazy." *New Yorker,* September 23, 2002, 64.

Collins, Jim, and Jerry I. Porras. *Built to Last: Successful Habits of Visionary Companies.* New York: HarperCollins, 2002.

Craig, Susanne, and John Hechinger. "Regulators Find Problem Trading at Edward Jones." *Wall Street Journal,* December 29, 2004.

Crook, Clive. "The Good Company: A Survey of Corporate Responsibility." *The Economist,* January 22, 2005, 3–6.

Dore, Ronald. *Stock Market Capitalism, Welfare Capitalism: Japan and Germany versus the Anglo-Saxons.* New York: Oxford University Press, 2000.

Eichenwald, Kurt. *Conspiracy of Fools: A True Story.* New York: Random House, 2005.

———. "Reform Effort at Businesses Feels Pressure." *New York Times*, January 14, 2005.

Eisinger, Jesse. "Follow the CEO's Money." *Wall Street Journal*, March 1, 2005.

Ellison, Sarah, and Eric Bellman. "Clean Water, No Profit." *Wall Street Journal*, February 23, 2005.

Farkas, Steve, Ann Duffett, and Jean Johnson, with Beth Syat. *A Few Bad Apples? An Exploratory Look at What Typical Americans Think about Business Ethics Today*. New York: Public Agenda, 2004.

"Fat Cats Turn to Low Fat." *The Economist*, March 5, 2005, 14.

Ferguson, Niall. *Colossus: The Price of American Empire*. New York: Penguin, 2004.

Garfinkle, Norton. "The Future of the American Dream: The Fight for a Productive Middle Class Economy." In *Uniting America: Restoring the Vital Center to American Democracy*, ed. Norton Garfinkle and Daniel Yankelovich. New Haven: Yale University Press, 2006.

Garten, Jeffrey E., ed. *World View: Global Strategies for the New Economy*. Boston: Harvard Business School Press, 1994.

Glater, Jonathan D. "Sorry, I'm Keeping the Bonus Anyway." *New York Times*, March 13, 2005.

Gourevitch, Peter A., and James Shinn. *Political Power and Corporate Control: The New Global Politics of Corporate Governance*. Princeton: Princeton University Press, 2005.

Gunther, Marc. *Faith and Fortune: The Quiet Revolution to Reform American Business*. New York: Crown Business, 2004.

Hakim, Danny. "G.M. to Seek Cuts in Union Health Benefits." *New York Times*, March 24, 2005.

Hamel, Gary. *Leading the Revolution*. Boston: Harvard Business School Press, 2000.

Harman, Sidney. *Mind Your Own Business: A Maverick's Guide to Business, Leadership, and Life*. New York: Currency/Doubleday, 2003.

Heilbroner, Robert. *21st Century Capitalism*. New York: Norton, 1993.

Hesselbein, Frances, Marshall Goldsmith, and Iain Somerville, eds. *Leading for Innovation and Organizing for Results*. San Francisco: Jossey-Bass, 2002.

Jackson, Ira A., and Jane Nelson. *Profits with Principles: Seven Strategies for Delivering Value with Values*. New York: Currency/Doubleday, 2004.

Jensen, Michael C. "Value Maximization, Stakeholder Theory, and the Corporate Objective Function." *Journal of Applied Corporate Finance* 14, no. 3 (2001): 8–21.

Kotler, Philip, and Nancy Lee. *Corporate Social Responsibility: Doing the Most Good for Your Company and Your Cause*. Hoboken, N.J.: Wiley, 2005.

Kotter, John P. *Leading Change.* Boston: Harvard Business School Press, 1996.

Lorsch, Jay W., Leslie Berlowitz, and Andy Zelleke, eds. *Restoring Trust in American Business.* Cambridge: MIT Press, 2005.

"Market Dangers." *Wall Street Week with Fortune.* PBS Television. KPBS, San Diego, December 24, 2004.

Morgenson, Gretchen. "Markets May Rebound, but Distrust Remains." *New York Times,* September 8, 2002.

Nadler, David A., with Mark B. Nadler. *Champions of Change: How CEOs and Their Companies Are Mastering the Skills of Radical Change.* San Francisco: Jossey-Bass, 1998.

Pepper, John. *What Really Matters.* Procter and Gamble, 2005.

Peterson, Peter G. "A Personal Postscript." *The Conference Board Commission on Public Trust and Private Enterprise.* New York: Conference Board, 2002.

Public Agenda. *For Goodness' Sake: Why So Many Americans Want Religion to Play a Greater Role in Public Life.* New York: Public Agenda, 2001.

Rajan, Raghuram, and Luigi Zingales. "The Great Reversals: The Politics of Financial Development in the Twentieth Century." *Journal of Financial Economics* 69 (2003): 5–50.

Roe, Mark. *Political Determinants of Corporate Governance: Political Context, Corporate Impact.* New York: Oxford University Press, 2002.

Roner, Lisa. "U.S. Pharmaceutical Industry Ethics Rated Higher by Executives Than Public." *Ethical Corporation.* http://www.ethicalcorp.com/content_print.asp?ContentID=3541

Rubin, Robert E., and Jacob Weisberg. *In an Uncertain World: Tough Choices from Wall Street to Washington.* New York: Random House, 2003.

Schwartz, Peter, and Peter Leyden. "The Long Boom." *Wired,* July 1997, 116+.

Scott, Lee. "Wal-Mart's Impact on Society: A Key Moment in Time for American Capitalism." *New York Review of Books,* April 7, 2005, 6–7.

Senge, Peter, Art Kleiner, Charlotte Roberts, Richard Ross, and Bryan Smith, eds. *The Fifth Discipline Fieldbook: Strategies and Tools for Building a Learning Organization.* New York: Currency/Doubleday, 1994.

Shellenberger, Michael, and Ted Nordhaus. "The Death of Environmentalism: Global warming Politics in a PostEnvironmental World." September 29, 2004. http://www.thebreakthrough.org/images/Death_of_Environmentalism.pdf

Smith, Adam. *An Inquiry into the Nature and Causes of the Wealth of Nations.* 1776.

Toqueville, Alexis de. *Democracy in America.* Cambridge: Sever and Francis, 1862.

Viewpoint Learning, Inc. "Essentials for Leading Knowledge Workers." Presentation, April 2003.

Welch, Jack, with John A. Byrne. *Jack: Straight from the Gut.* New York: Warner Business, 2001.

Whitehead, Alfred North. "On Foresight." Delivered to the Graduate School of Business Administration, Harvard University, 1930.

Yankelovich, Daniel. "Corporate Logic in the 1990s." Arthur W. Page Society Spring Seminar, 1994.

———. "DYG SCAN 2004: Getting Beyond Polarization to Common Ground." Presented at DYG West Coast Conference,.

———. "DYG SCAN 2005: How Converging Trends Created the Business Scandals and What to Do about Them." Presented at DYG West Coast Conference, March 18, 2005.

———. "The Growing Centrality of Trust." Presented to Toyota/Blackstone, July 26, 2002.

———. *The Magic of Dialogue: Transforming Conflict into Cooperation.* New York: Simon and Schuster, 1999.

———. *New Rules: Searching for Self-Fulfillment in a World Turned Upside Down.* New York: Random House, 1981.

———. "Screwed Again." Presented to YPO, November 21, 2002.

Yankelovich, Daniel, and Steven Rosell. "Taking Leadership/Building Trust." Presented to the North American Summit on Public Engagement, November 10, 2004.

———. "Making Trust a Competitive Asset: Breaking Out of Narrow Frameworks." Report of the Special Meeting of Senior Executives on the Deeper Crisis of Trust, May 15–17, 2003.

Yankelovich, Daniel, and Viewpoint Learning, Inc. "The Employee-Owned Company in a Climate of Mistrust." Presented to the NCEO/Beyster Employee Ownership Conference, March 27, 2003.

Index